REFERENCE

33 SONNETS OF THE RESISTANCE
AND OTHER POEMS

33 SONNETS COMPOSÉS AU SECRET
ET AUTRES POÈMES

Jean Cassou

33 Sonnets of the Resistance

and other poems

33 SONNETS COMPOSÉS AU SECRET
ET AUTRES POÈMES

Translated by Timothy Adès
Introduced by Alistair Elliot

'Visible Poets' No. 7

Arc Publications
2002

Published by Arc Publications, Nanholme Mill,
Shaw Wood Road, Todmorden, Lancs OL14 6DA, UK

Design by Tony Ward
Printed at the Arc & Throstle Press Ltd
Nanholme Mill, Shaw Wood Road, Todmorden
Lancs OL14 6DA, UK

ISBN 1 900072 89 0

The publishers acknowledge financial assistance from
Yorkshire Arts Board.

ACKNOWLEDGEMENTS AND NOTES

These English translations of the 33 Sonnets, with their Introduction, appeared in *Comparative Criticism no. 19* (Cambridge University Press), having been placed equal first in the BCLA/BCLT Translation Competition, 1995/6. In addition, some of the English versions in the present volume have appeared in *Modern Poetry in Translation*, and in *Outposts*.

Five of Cassou's poems, with English text by Timothy Adès, appeared in *Translation and Literature*, 1997.

Jean Cassou's original French text of *Trente-trois sonnets composés au secret*, with Aragon's complete introduction, was re-published by Éditions Gallimard in 1995. The Gallimard volume also contains all the thirty-one poems of *La Rose et le Vin*, complete with Cassou's commentary.

Jean Cassou's work is reproduced here with grateful acknowledgements to Éditions Gallimard for the above works, and to Mme Isabelle Jan for all the remainder; the source for these is Jean Cassou, *Oeuvre Lyrique / Das Lyrische Werk*, published by Erker (St Gallen) in 1971, a bilingual edition with full German text, in rhyme and metre where applicable.

A full documentation of Cassou appears in the catalogue of an exhibition, *Jean Cassou: Un Musée Imaginé*, shown in 1995, with support from the Centre Georges Pompidou, at the Bibliothèque Nationale, France. There are studies of the poetry in both Gallimard and the catalogue, by Florence de Lussy. See also Jean Cassou by Pierre Georgel, in *Les Poètes d'Aujourd'hui*, Seghers, 1967.

Arc Publications: 'Visible Poets' Series
Series Editor: Jean Boase-Beier

CONTENTS

33 SONNETS

Poems from THE ROSE AND THE WINE

OTHER POEMS

SERIES EDITOR'S NOTE

There is a prevailing view of translated poetry, especially in England, which maintains that it should read as though it had originally been written in English. The books in the 'Visible Poets' series aim to challenge that view. They assume that the reader of poetry is by definition someone who wants to experience the strange, the unusual, the new, the foreign, someone who delights in the stretching and distortion of language which makes any poetry, translated or not, alive and distinctive. The translators of the poets in this series aim not to hide but to reveal the original, to make it visible and, in so doing, to render visible the translator's task too. The reader is invited not only to experience the unique fusion of the creative talents of poet and translator embodied in the English poems in these collections, but also to speculate on the processes of their creation and so to gain a deeper understanding and enjoyment of both original and translated poems.

Jean Boase-Beier

TRANSLATOR'S PREFACE

Several years after translating the 33 Sonnets and their introduction, I am still in awe of them. I am only a translator, I do not live or think on the epic scale of John Black and Francis Anger, to give them their underground names. Translating is like acting. Over a period, I play a variety of roles, without being identified with one or another.

Translation theorists tend to ask, How do you translate poetry? But the real question, even for translators, is, How do you write or compose poetry? At any rate that is the case in this particular series. And there is probably no answer.

When I tell someone I translate poetry, I am usually asked, from what language, and I may say French, Spanish, German ... most of the work is at the English end. They ask, Do you write your own poetry? and I say, when I translate a poem, you get a poem. I rely on a proper poet, who is usually dead and has passed the test of time, who takes care of style, content and all; I am just the wren, or possibly the small primate, on the eagle's back. I sight a passing poem far out at sea and, with our English word-horde as a peaceful escort, bring it to safe harbour in home waters. It's not that easy; often I am ignominiously beaten off, having barely scratched a line. I like bilingual editions, by which all of us who are halfway competent can receive a poem in stereo. I prefer to work with rhyme and metre, which, being obviously impossible, paradoxically gives me a freedom denied to the exponents of free verse who must remain slaves to the original.

As for Jean Cassou, it started, as usual, with one poem in an anthology: Sonnet XXIII. At the library I copied out most of the sonnets in pencil, as required. For months they were my secret hobby, for I had not yet emerged as a poetry translator. Only at the end did I read Aragon's blazing Introduction and realise that, in the title, 'Au Secret' means not 'In Secret' but 'While Being Held Incomunicado', and that Sonnet XV has thirteen syllables to the line. Still later I discovered that Sonnet XXVII, which I thought was addressed to the invader (as I think XVII is, and perhaps XIII too), was in fact addressed to Cassou's friend Joë Bousquet. My version stands unaltered: Cassou can be fairly strange and obscure. As for the other poems in this volume, they are simply poems that caught my eye, there is no principle of selection. Cassou's free verse, and the long commentaries of *The Rose and the Wine*, are under-represented here.

The editorial rubric of this series has prompted some thought. A poem does not have to be a translation to use strange and unusual language. Nor does a translated poem need to use strange language in order to transmit something of a foreign culture: it suffices that the content of the poem is culturally foreign, in which case (if not in all cases) the translation may as well sound like a work written in English. Aragon hears in the 33 Sonnets 'the voice of France herself'. They are culturally foreign to most of us because today's English-speaking peoples have mostly not been occupied by such a regime. We can taste this largely continental experience of occupation, through Cassou's poems, without requiring our English version to be flavoured with French idiom. Cassou did not merely live under an occupation; he resisted. His personal experience was rare and special, because most people in the occupied countries did not join the Resistance, or go to prison. Most did not choose to, many did not have the chance. This Resistance man's human sympathy and impenetrable resilience were lifelong qualities that persist all through his poems. Finally Cassou was well-read in French and other literatures, and all his poetry must be full of French echoes and some others which might be seen as strange; but any such overtones, if they are not from our common patrimony, the classics and scriptures for example, will not re-echo in an English version, belonging instead in the commentary or footnotes.

Film-makers face a similar linguistic choice between the straight and the strange. In a well-crafted comic British TV series set in occupied France, the French characters spoke English with a strong French accent; in a serious treatment today, whether Hollywood or art-house, they would just speak French, perhaps with subtitles, or plain English. Shakespeare's characters, be they Danes, Romans, Greeks or Celts, all speak an English of Shakespearean virtuosity which in no way acknowledges the characters' native tongues. (I deliberately name peoples whose own languages have helped to make English what it is.) Likewise Homer's Trojans speak the same magnificent Greek as his Greeks. It would be a travesty to read our editorial rubric as implying that the way of the comic TV series is the only correct one. I prefer to read it as saying that, just as foreign ideas and contacts may sometimes jog us out of our set ways, so the translation of poetry may be the occasion of combating the lingering notion that our poetry should be more prosaic than our prose.

For myself, whether or not I endorse any of these aims, the

path to achieving a satisfactory translation with rhyme and metre is so narrow and tortuous that I can hardly afford to take them into account. My good fortune is to bring the reader something of what Aragon called 'the high water mark of the great drama of France'.

Timothy Adès

INTRODUCTION

The name of Jean Cassou (1897-1986) does not appear in anthologies of twentieth-century French verse on either side of the Channel. But it should, for the thirty-three sonnets he composed in a Vichy prison between December 13th 1941 and February 1942 are a phenomenon of great interest. They were nearly all composed in the dark, half a sonnet per night, committed to memory, and only written down when a few days before his provisional release he was allowed some books, a pencil and some sheets of paper. The quality of the sonnets is variable, but the best of them are very fine, and one cannot help connecting their failure to make it into fame with the politics of their author: although the poems were published (clandestinely) with a rousing patriotic preface by Aragon at the beginning of 1944, Cassou rejected communism in 1949 and was then 'dragged through the mud' and 'abandoned by most of his friends'. One may deduce that he was too open-minded and independent to please the old comrades who dominated the Paris intelligentsia for so many years. Even his service in the Resistance (including over a year in prison) and his being left for dead by the Germans in the night of the liberation of Toulouse were no longer recommendation enough.

It is not of course unprecedented in modern times for poets to compose without writing materials – one thinks of Wordsworth and Milton – and poets have also been able to compose lines in prison, though usually able to write their work down as it forms; but I can think of only one other case like that of Cassou: Solzhenitsyn composed in his head, and memorised, a long poem in ballad form when arrested and jailed (also by his own countrymen) a few years later in the same war. But Cassou's sonnets are a quite different sort of composition from Solzhenitsyn's narrative of war; securely in the formal literary tradition, somewhat surrealist, at a distance from clear prosaic statement (as Nerval's sonnet 'El Desdichado' is) but referring somewhat abstractly to the crude circumstances of captivity, personal, but almost self-censored as if the jailers could find and read them, they are a fascinating series of strongly emotional linked mood-pictures and memories.

Technically Cassou's sonnets are surprising, considering they grew up so nakedly in the field of short-term memory. They obey the rules of versification but break them in the modern way with odd rhymes (consolés, lavées, forêt, jugée; froid, frimas; froide, malade; and so on) and odd rhythms, sometimes counting the mute e and sometimes not; they also have various line lengths, even in the same sonnet, and sonnet XV is written in alexandrins with an extra syllable.

But these poems are not only interesting in their cloudy relation to events and to the symbolist masters of their form. They also have the mysterious quality that I prize in favourite English poems: their point is not blunted at one reading, they come to mind now and then later and demand to be re-read, they grow and explain themselves and each other as they become familiar. There are beautiful sonnets about the sounds of the outside and the stars of inner darkness (VI), Paris in time of love, again with free street-noises rising (XXV), premonitions in the midst of summer happiness (fears of approaching war or perhaps of the end of love) (X), even an address apparently to the invader (XIII) and what I take to be an obscure reference to the swastika (XXXI). There is also, remarkably, a translation of a Hofmannsthal sonnet (IX) which found its way to Cassou's cell on a leaf of the occupying power's German-language Paris newspaper. (Aragon treated this as a gesture towards a cultured and humane Germany beyond the reach of Cassou's jailers and their Nazi bosses.)

It is not known whether the arrangement of the sonnets is in the chronological order of their composition, but the first one reads as if it recorded the experience of the narrator's first night in a jail from which he might never emerge. A funeral ship glides forward without sails (the low cell like a coffin floating on the current of time); on it lies a horizontal voyager (the Viking of this funeral), moving somewhere, without control, in the dark. The poem seems also to hint at the traveller's psychological condition: he seems to be considering suicide when he says (literally), 'shall I try tonight the royal game, reverse the flow, and stand up' (to brain myself on the low ceiling)? Finally, the last three lines have the smooth patina of a Valéry or a Nerval but they describe a howl of despair: a cry that is, literally again, 'like the soul of a dog'. It is a majestic performance indeed, the essence of an experience whose details we long (in vain) to know more about, but which are characteristically veiled and unexplained. These private sentiments and private losses (who is the child Alice-Abeille of sonnet III?) resonate as if with the trauma of the French nation of that time, captured, in shock, and facing a future darkened not only by the bestiality of the conquerors but by the complicity of some of its own leaders in their horrible whims. All the same, what is described is the shudder of a reviving spirit, a spirit of, precisely, resistance to the 'cadavre en moi'.

After the war Cassou had a distinguished career as an art historian and museum director, but somehow managed to find time to continue writing novels (as he had done before the war) and verse, some of which is presented here. However, it seems to me that the conditions of those two months in prison and perhaps the immediate threat of death helped produce a concentration of his linguistic powers that he was never to approach again. And perhaps it may be added that the formal suit of the sonnet, the lyric poet's party best, may have been an essential aid to him in that dark time.

Translating these poems must have been hard. Tim Adès has produced excellent versions which rhyme and scan if the originals do, and without altogether dispelling the symbolist multitude of meanings in many of the poems, are also helpful interpretations, as well as keeping much of the magnificence that makes some of these poems striking. Of course the reader will want to argue with some of those interpretations; but that, we may say, is inevitable, part of the problem and the beauty of it.

Alistair Elliot

INTRODUCTION (1962) by Jean Cassou

I was arrested for Resistance activity by the Vichy police on 13 December 1941, at Toulouse in the Unoccupied Zone, and held incomunicado at the Toulouse military prison, with the other comrades of our network who were brought in with me. I was not in solitary confinement, strictly speaking, since the prisons were full, and we found ourselves sharing the same cell between two. (My companion, Fernand Bernard, was later transferred to Eysses prison and took part in the prison revolt there; after a night of fighting, the resisters had to surrender and Darnand, arriving with his militia force, gave the order for those responsible for the riot to be shot. The wounded Bernard had to be tied to the stake, and he and his companions died singing the Marseillaise.)

Even so, all the other conditions of solitary confinement were realised: no exercise walks round the yard, no visits, no paper to write on, no correspondence, and nothing to read. When evening came we would throw ourselves down on our mattresses and try to sleep despite the cold. From the first night, as a way of passing the time, I worked at composing sonnets in my head, this strict prosodic form striking me as the one best suited to an exercise in composition which involved pure brainwork and memory.

In February I was provisionally set free with two comrades; some days earlier, our lawyers had gained us the right to receive books and to have the use of a pencil and some sheets of paper. Among the books I was sent was an anthology of Latin poetry, which explains the quotation over Sonnet XVI; and I was able to jot down the sonnets which I had already composed, that is to say nearly all. For those two months I had composed half a sonnet a night. Later, when our network was scheduled to appear before the French military tribunal of the 17th Division on 30th July 1942, I debated with my two comrades in provisional freedom, Fausto Nitti and Marcel Vanhove, whether we would appear before the tribunal or go to ground. We decided to appear, so as not to cause problems for our comrades still in prison, and to maintain our joint defence with them as prepared by our lawyers. I was sentenced to a year in prison: I served out my remaining time, and then resumed my service in the Resistance.

Meanwhile I had passed my 33 Sonnets to Éditions de Minuit who published them under cover early in 1944, under the name of Jean Noir on Aragon's advice, and with a preface by him, signed François La Colère. An admirably warm and generous preface, alive with all the passion that fraternally united the writers of France in those wretched times.

This book was then brought out by Cahiers du Rhône: distribution of their edition was taken over by Éditions de Minuit, the original publishers, who normalised the book by giving the writers their real names; then Limes Verlag, Wiesbaden (1957) in the German translation of Franz von Rexroth, with facing text in French.

In the famous phrase, all poetry is poetry of circumstances. Those in which I composed my sonnets are certainly the best possible for providing a poet with a pure and complete experience of poetic creation. All we imprisoned poets agree that we have enjoyed a rare privilege; except that some have done so only during the experience itself, and without having, as I had, the additional good fortune of seeing the results in public later on.

FROM THE INTRODUCTION BY LOUIS ARAGON ('François La Colère'), 1944

The manuscript I have before me is headed '33 Sonnets composés au secret' and dedicated 'À mes compagnons de prisons.' It may at first seem difficult to discuss, since I cannot benefit from knowing the author, and must say nothing about that before the time is ripe: I cannot deploy the critical technique which puts a piece of writing alongside others, already known, from the same hand. He calls himself Jean Noir and I must leave it at that.

'33 Sonnets composés au secret' ... This much, though, I can surely say: the sonnet, this peculiar cerebral and poetic challenge, was polished for four centuries by the most skilful lyric writers, and seemed to be at its zenith with Mallarmé; and yet it returns to us at this most unexpected moment, when we thought it must be worn out with refinement and old age: and in a strange place and manner, with a new magnificence. The sonnet returns to us from the night of the dungeons: not an academic sonnet fathered in leisured seclusion, but a sonnet inscribed in the mysterious line of the intimations of France: the rightful place for a writer and a poet who is not some improvising rhymer but a man whose inner being needed only to know that dismal cell in which our France finds herself imprisoned: a man entirely predestined to be here as the palpable echo of a deeper world, since ... and I was about to mention all the thrilling insight in the work of this man who must remain anonymous, in that flowing river, manifested here again, that ran through the embattled heart of our people at every stage of Liberty, that sustained the *misérables*, and those June martyrs whom the young Flaubert saw fettered in Paris, and those who refused the armistice of '71 and sang 'Le Temps des Cerises': that current which animates the deep springs of a truly French art, the work of an artist; for among the writers of our country there are few who are precisely *artists*, as he is: and in all his writings, Jean Noir, even when he most seems to avoid the common thoroughfares, always sounds a popular groundswell, as when a cultured song recalls a twopenny refrain: and this singular duality is also like the reflection of another duality, between this man you might run into, whose hand I shook, whose name was in the telephone directory, and the different person that this book reveals, who may grow grey but will for ever be a young, ardent, passionate being, whether with the ladies or with *la patrie*: and I could explain Jean Noir only by comparisons with music, Chopin or Mozart, no, that's not it, the hidden fire, the openness to tragic events ... yes, it has all been as if his life has concealed the true nature that his books disclose, and which made of him from that first hour in June 1940 the soldier who refused the armistice, like his private heroes: the soldier of the Liberation ... but I was forgetting that I am here to discuss the sonnet, and nothing more.

It was not mere chance that led this prisoner in his cell to choose the sonnet, and a sonnet which may have taken its Nervalian tone from the stone walls of the prison. (Un pur esprit s'accroît sous l'écorce des pierres). He had no writing materials, this prisoner, save only time and his mental faculties. He had only the night for his ink, only memory for his paper. He had to hold the poem up, as one might hold up a child out of the water. He had to hold it until the uncertain day of his release from prison. He had to do more than write it, he had to learn it. The fourteen lines of the sonnet, their perfect interconnection, the mnemonic value of their rhymes, all this imposed on the poet, not the acrobatic problem solved by such as Voiture, but the necessary framework to link his outward circumstances to his interior life. From now on it will be almost impossible not to see in the sonnet the expression of freedom under constraint, the embodiment of thought in fetters. How could we not have known? '33 Sonnets composés au secret' ... In the most recondite poetry, at the limits of history, a peerless document of man and his dreams, and, in chains, of that which cannot be chained.

I shall say of these sonnets that they are poignant and inaccessible, and yet direct and uncontrived. I shall speak of these sonnets for those who long to learn more about the man, and so might be in danger of closing this volume without sensing this low murmur of ourselves, without recognising this deep-buried fire ...

I shall say of these sonnets that not only are they born in fetters, but they are the negation of those fetters; and not only is the poet a son of France, but in these poems can be heard singing, too, the voice of France herself. And I beseech you to hear it.

***

Oh! ce soir soit pour nous le dernier soir tombé,
et puisqu'il faut rêver, rêvons la mort des rêves.

Let us now see no further evenings fall:
since we must dream, let's dream that dreams must die.

The survivor of a shipwreck is expected to characterise the horror in a way which is beyond the range of anyone who has not seen the waves overwhelm the bridge, and the agonising choice of those who go off in the lifeboat and those who remain on board. A John Milton, for example, is permitted to convey the dark night of blindness in *Paradise Lost.* The poet is besieged by an audience avid to hear it all, both in description and in symbolism, just as they imagine it; and the result may be, given the unexpected grandeur of his private intentions, that they are terribly disappointed.

If what you expect from this poet is prison poetry, the description of the life led there, even the cries that go up from dungeons of stone, then you will simply be left holding these sonnets, like children with pretty shells, not knowing how to hear the sea inside them. Perhaps also you hope to find words in praise of those values for which this man was deprived of his freedom. As you enter this hell, abandon that hope, too.

... since we must dream, let's dream that dreams must die.

The prisoner enveloped in darkness is far from content to bear witness to hunger, thirst, cold, the pain of indignity and humiliation. The poem is his great act of defiance of the contempt that he suffers. The poem is his superhuman effort to continue as a human being, to reach those regions of mind and heart which everything around him denies and debases. The poem – the sonnet – is not a running away, an evasion in the fashionable term of modern criticism, and this term takes on here an equivocal and mocking tone; it is his reply, the grandiloquent reply of a man in the hands of pygmies, a Gulliver resurgent in the nets of Lilliput. Its beauty, its power, and its disturbing message come precisely from the *gigantic* gap between this deprived individual sitting by a squalid slop-bucket in that dark night of wretchedness, insulted and ordered about by brutes at their pleasure: the gigantic gap there is, the contrast between this individual deprived of his being and the purity of his inner universe, which, as these sonnets show, nothing can snatch away from him. (At this point it will be clear why I dwelt on the example of my friend at Gurs who taught his companions the origins of the French language: compare him with Jean Noir, making up these sonnets in his head, and both of them cease to be the exception, the disconcerting fact, both provide the human solution to a superhuman problem, both appear as the very exemplars of our dignity in misfortune. They both do so, because there is the same gap between their circumstances and their paradoxical choice of activity. And the second example helps me deny the quality of 'running away' by which some people might seek to account for Jean Noir.)

> ... since we must dream, let's dream that dreams must die.

As to the relative obscurity of these sonnets, there are several points to be made. Obscure as the soliloquy of one who is not addressing some improbable listener, but bearing witness to himself and himself alone; obscure, too, as dreams but especially as the thoughts of insomnia, obscure as smoky diamonds which nonetheless have all the fire of the others, obscure initially as the final pain which becomes explicit ... In his cell when total night has descended, what chimeras, monsters and splendours inhabit the prisoner? Thoughts, memories, in which the myths of this man's destiny intersect; and the future is opposed and compared to the past. Sometimes a surprising image shines out among these murky boughs:

> Il n'y avait que des troncs déchirés
> que couronnaient des vols de corbeaux ivres,
> et le château était couvert de givre,
> ce soir de fer où je m'y présentai ...

Only torn tree-trunks; drunken flight
of crows above them; that was all:
thick frost lay on the castle wall
when I walked in, that iron night ...

or this morsel of another vision:

Lorsque nous entrerons dans cette ville chinoise
je boiterai un peu, mais je connaîtrai l'amour

When we pass through the Chinese city-gates
I'll stumble, but I'll be alive to love,

both of which may owe their peculiarity to the unexpected use, amid alexandrines, of verses of ten and thirteen syllables; unless one can think the very character of the vision compelled the poet to change his metre. For it would be absurd to see no more in these sonnets than the outcome of those nights of captivity: they are also a drawing-out of linguistic skill and poetic meditation by a craftsman of verse, a proven master of the modern handling of antique metre: and we must mention how far he goes in rhyming, at the limits of assonance, and his systematic taste for the weak rhyme, often combined with a rare word; and a way, too, of bringing in colloquial words and idiomatic makeweights (a donc which the unsuspecting might see as a filler, when it is the whole beauty of the line, and of the stress); and the high point of my proposition is perhaps that moment when he takes a poem of Hugo von Hofmannsthal ... but, for this story, we need to stop.

A sonnet of Hofmannsthal. A German sonnet, to which the patriot in the shadowy depths will give its French expression. Let no-one tell me that this confrontation of the nations is excessive: on the contrary, it is what gives this episode its unexpected value. Below the translation there is a commentary, since, for once, the captive found he could not do without a commentary:

(The prisoners were forbidden anything to read. One day, though, a fragment of an issue of the *Pariser Zeitung* came into my hands. My cellmate and I devoured the evil print which was at any rate something to read. I had the joy of lighting on a sonnet of Hofmannsthal: 'Die Beiden', a famous piece from the anthologies which had always charmed me and which I adapted into our language by great efforts during one of my nights of insomnia).

One will not quickly forget this intellectual adventure at the heart of the most terrible of wars: this moment of reunion ... put Jean Noir and Hofmannsthal in prison and two poets fraternise, with all the burden of condemnation that rests on this accord beyond and outside their loyalties, against their gaolers and that Germany which their gaolers obey. One will not quickly forget this adventure, pregnant with all the future, where the French part is sustained with its double splendour of moderation and excess, which charges a sonnet so powerfully that my sentence explodes, founders, drunk with a national pride whose ingredients are courage, incomparable poetry and resolve, and that loftiness of spirit that makes our poets the equals of our heroes. I imagine it was pride pure and simple that night which filled him, a man who was in prison for resisting the Germans, and yet marvellously translated Hofmannsthal in his prison. I can imagine his feelings, and by doing so I know much more than I would from a faithful report of the indomitable character of the French in captivity. I learn from this what no-one, not even this poet of ours, would presume to relate. I understand, beyond his modesty, beyond that reserve always maintained by those who have touched the pit of horror, I understand the mechanism which has come into play so often in these inexpiable years, which will amaze the world with our martyrs, this harvest of heroism, this unbelievable profusion of magnificent lives and deaths, which give today's France a hundred or a thousand times that which sufficed to make the grandeur of Rome. I understand by this anecdote of the translated sonnet the greatness of our heroes, their simplicity, even their silence. One will not quickly forget this intellectual adventure.

Whoever sees, in these '33 Sonnets composés au secret', only the awakened musings, the flashes of lightning, the images formed behind the eyelids like a negation of fetters, has not known, any more than the child I spoke of, how to hear the sea in those fine and fantastic shells gathered on unfamiliar beaches. It all happens as I described, and at the same time it all happens another way. The armoury of images, the vocabulary, the play of themes, all reflect the prison, that prison where a man is held in denial of man himself; dream, sleep and memory are all a cell of torment for the being of flesh and blood:

> ... since we must dream, let's dream that dreams must die.

(I repeat). And it is imperative to add to this soliloquy I mentioned, a reconstruction of its prison surroundings, so that every sonnet, taken and read as thought, pain, flame, a human being in captivity, will resound, if I put it to my ear, with that ocean roar which is the eternal record of liberty lost for the love of liberty:

> Life's distant sounds, celestial, tucked away:
> horns hooting, children going home to tea,
> the church bells pealing for a festal day,
> cars blindly heading for infinity,
>
> rumours – wrapped, muffled, swathed; what people say:
> demons of darkness and adversity
> have brought me to your chasm; who but they?
> I touch your friendly faces, haltingly.

The real world is humming, just beyond the drama of the walls; the real world that the prisoner makes out from the depth of his night, like that car hooter, and which illuminates time past and time future in such sonnets as XXI, XXII and XXIII: the tomb of the poet Antonio Machado who died on the threshold of France when his people were defeated, this sonnet of the workers, bleeding like workers' hands, and this reincarnation of 'Au Temps des Cerises' that ends with the cry:

> Stream forth, bright dawn of carnival,
> when fists have guns to spark the fray!

which without doubt is the common cry of all the captives of La Patrie, the cry of the French heart for which in our time every French breast is still a prison.

No, the prisoner did not shut his eyes to reality, but to the passing defeat he had suffered. If he shut his eyes, it was to see in them more clearly those flashes of anger and pain, to see the essential of a world in which the prison is a mere accident, an accessory, though a dreadful one. And in sonnet V there is a confession, a paraphrase of the poet's half-yielded secret, when he says:

> The poets shall return to earth one day ...
> ....
> They'll recognise in masks maniacal,
> dancing the farandole in carnival,
> their finest verse, freed from the agony
> that gave it birth ...

Perhaps the reader will have misunderstood my comment on those makeweight words on which the stress and beauty of these lines depend. What about that 'enfin' in the line

> leurs plus beaux vers enfin délivrés du sanglot
> their finest verse *freed (i.e. free at last)* from the agony

That enfin reveals to us the poet's aim. That enfin conceived in prison, conceived in isolation.

> ... and then, in happiness,
> as evening falls they shall depart, and bless
> long love and glory, wind, and blood, and sea.

For if the prisoner is dreaming "that dreams must die" in his own liberation, then well may his finest verse be *at last*

> ... freed from the agony
> that gave it birth ...

Let the prison crumble, and let only the poetry survive it! And that poetry, for all its imposed secrecy and solitude, will certainly outlive all our prisons, just as the ebbing of a great flood leaves those thrilling messages at which children tremble in amazement, which register the level that was once attained, with the date: the high water mark of the great drama of France. That poetry which perhaps really reaches its conclusion in the last sonnet but one:

> The outraged universe stores up redress ...
> ....
> Vengeance in heaven, total, no remorse!
> Yes, thunder soothes the fevered trees, no doubt;
> when you are judged, that silence shall be yours,
> the silence when the judged are blotted out ...
> ....
> When hate and scorn have shattered every wall,
> heart close to breaking, what remains at all
> but to hate hate, scorn scorn, no less?

And that, perhaps, in a few simple words, is the lesson France gives the world as she sits in her misfortune.

33 SONNETS OF THE RESISTANCE

33 SONNETS COMPOSÉS AU SECRET

I

La barque funéraire est, parmi les étoiles,
longue comme le songe et glisse sans voilure,
et le regard du voyageur horizontal
s'étale, nénuphar, au fil de l'aventure.

Cette nuit, vais-je enfin tenter le jeu royal,
renverser dans mes bras le fleuve qui murmure,
et me dresser, dans ce contour d'un linceul pâle
comme une tour qui croule aux bords des sépultures?

L'opacité, déjà, où je passe frissonne,
et comme si son nom était encor Personne,
tout mon cadavre en moi tressaille sous ses liens.

Je sens me parcourir et me ressusciter,
de mon front magnétique à la proue de mes pieds,
un cri silencieux, comme une âme de chien.

II

Mort à toute fortune, à l'espoir, à l'espace,
mais non point mort au temps qui pursuit sa moisson,
il me faut me retraire et lui céder la place,
mais dans ce dénuement grandit ma passion.

Je l'emporte avec moi dans un pays sans nom
où nuit et nuit sur nuit me pressent et m'effacent.
L'ombre y dévore l'ombre, et j'y dresse le front
à mesure qu'un mur de songe boit ma trace.

Ce n'est vie ni non plus néant. De ma veillée
les enfants nouveau-morts errent dans l'entre-deux.
Transparentes clartés, apparues, disparues,

élans sans avenir, souvenirs sans passé,
décroître fait leur joie, expirer fait leur jeu,
et Psyché brûle en eux, les ailes étendues.

I

The funerary ship on starry ways
glides on, as long as thought, with no sails spread;
the traveller, laid out, unfolds his gaze,
a water-lily on adventure's thread.

Is this the night I try the game of kings,
embrace and overturn the plangent waves,
and rise up in my deathly bandagings,
a tower crumbling at the brink of graves?

Now, where I tread, the dark reverberates.
My corpse, confined inside me, palpitates;
yes, I could still be known as Nobody.

I feel, renewing, surging at my prow,
back from my feet to my magnetic brow,
like a dog's vital spark, a silent cry.

II

Dead to all fortune and to hope and space,
but not to time whose fullness is to be,
I must draw back, leave time to set the pace;
my passion deepens in this penury.

I take it with me to a nameless place
where night and night on night bear down on me.
Shadow eats shadow there. I show my face;
my tracks are drowned in mental masonry.

Not life, not nothingness. I cannot sleep:
in no-man's-land my new-dead children stray.
Now here, now vanished, lucid shimmerings,

memories of no past, a forward leap
to nowhere; dearth's their joy and death's their play,
and Psyche burns in them with outspread wings.

III

Je m'égare par les pics neigeux que mon front
recèle dans l'azur noir de son labyrinthe.
Plus d'autre route à moi ne s'ouvre, vagabond
enfoncé sous la voûte de sa propre plainte.

Errer dans ce lacis et délirer! Ô saintes
rêveries de la captivité. Les prisons
sont en moi mes prisonnières et dans l'empreinte
de mes profonds miroirs se font et se défont.

Je suis perdu si haut que l'on entend à peine
mon sourd appel comme un chiffon du ciel qui traîne.
Mais là-bas, clair pays d'où montent les matins,

dans ta prairie, Alice-Abeille, ma bergère,
si quelque voix, tout bas, murmure: «C'est ton père»,
va-t'en vers la montagne et prends-moi par la main.

IV

J'ai rêvé que je vous portais entre mes bras,
depuis la cour jusqu'à votre salon obscur.
Vous sembliez une sœur des chères créatures
que j'adore, mais je ne vous connaissais pas.

Il faisait une nuit de lune et de frimas,
une nuit de la vie, sonore d'aventures.
Tandis que je cherchais à voir votre figure,
je vous sentais légère et tremblante de froid.

Puis je vous ai perdue comme tant d'autres choses,
la perle des secrets et le safran des roses,
que le songe ou la terre offrirent à mon cœur.

Signes de ma mémoire, énigmes, tout me mène,
avec chaque soleil formé à si grand-peine,
au chef-d'œuvre d'un fort et lucide malheur.

III

I roam white peaks that my conniving brow
embezzles in its labyrinth's black sky.
No other road is open to me now,
a tramp thrust deep inside my own sad cry.

Blest prison-dreams! To wander in this maze:
to rave. Jails are the jailbirds I contain.
In my deep mirrors where each image stays,
they come and go, form and dissolve again.

I'm lost so high up that my muffled call,
trailed rag of cloud, is hardly audible.
Below, where dawn breaks on the shining land,

my sheepgirl in your meadow, Alice-Bee,
if a voice says 'Your father' quietly,
go to the mountainside and take my hand.

IV

I dreamed that in my arms I carried you
up from the courtyard to your room, lit low.
You seemed a sister of that darling crew
I love, but you were one I did not know.

It was a night of frost, a moonlit night,
a night of life, romantic, ringing, bold.
I tried to see your face, and you were cold,
you shivered to my touch, and you were light.

And then I lost you, lost like so much more,
saffron of roses, pearl of secret store,
that earth or dream had offered to my soul.

Riddles, remembered signs, bring back to me,
with every sun that forms so painfully,
this culminating, strong, transparent hell.

V

Les poètes, un jour, reviendront sur la terre.
Ils reverront le lac et la grotte enchantée,
les jeux d'enfants dans les bocages de Cythère,
le vallon des aveux, la maison des péchés,

et toutes les amies perdues dans la pensée,
les sœurs plaintives et les femmes étrangères,
le bonheur féerique et la douce fierté
qui posait des baisers à leur front solitaire.

Et ils reconnaîtront, sous des masques de folles,
à travers Carnaval, dansant la farandole,
leurs plus beaux vers enfin délivrés du sanglot

qui les fit naître. Alors, satisfaits, dans le soir,
ils s'en retourneront en bénissant la gloire,
l'amour perpétuel, le vent, le sang, les flots.

VI

Bruits lointains de la vie, divinités secrètes,
trompe d'auto, cris des enfants à la sortie,
carillon du salut à la veille des fêtes,
voiture aveugle se perdant à l'infini,

rumeurs cachées aux plis des épaisseurs muettes,
quels génies autres que l'infortune et la nuit
auraient su me conduire à l'abîme où vous êtes?
Et je touche à tâtons vos visages amis.

Pour mériter l'acceuil d'aussi profonds mystères
je me suis dépouillé de toute ma lumière:
la lumière aussitôt se cueille dans vos voix.

Qu'on me laisse à present repasser la poterne
et remonter, portant ces reflets noirs en moi,
fleurs d'un ciel inversé, astres de ma caverne.

V

The poets shall return to earth one day:
the lake and magic cave again they'll see,
Cythera's tanglewoods where children play,
the house of sins, the vale of constancy,

and, lost in meditation, every she,
sisters of sighs, fair friends from far away,
unearthly joy and sweet nobility
that kissed their forehead's loneliness away.

They'll recognise in masks maniacal,
dancing the farandole in carnival,
their finest verse, freed from the agony

that gave it birth: and then, in happiness,
as evening falls they shall depart, and bless
long love and glory, wind, and blood, and sea.

VI

Life's distant sounds, celestial, tucked away:
horns hooting, children going home to tea,
the church bells pealing for a festal day,
cars blindly heading for infinity,

rumours – wrapped, muffled, swathed; what people say:
demons of darkness and adversity
have brought me to your chasm; who but they?
I touch your friendly faces, haltingly.

Such depths of mystery! To earn the right
of welcome, I dispensed with all my light.
Your voice is heard; light quickly gathers there.

Let me bring back these star-signs from my cavern,
back through the postern-gate, and upward bear
black images, flowers from an inverse heaven.

VII

Bois cette tasse de ténèbres, et puis dors.
Nous prendrons ta misère ainsi qu'une couronne
et nous la porterons aux jardins de la mort.
Alors toi, comme un somnambule qui frissonne,

te glissant par la porte où ne passe personne,
tu t'en iras cueillir le myrte aux rameaux d'or.
Son éclat et celui de la rouge anémone,
dans la nuit rajeunie, te guideront aux bords

de la vraie vie et du pur accomplissement.
Là les songes sont sûrs, terribles et puissants.
Par le bleu matinal d'un éternel demain

ils viendront tous à ta rencontre, âme guérie,
et tu reconnaîtras, se tenant par la main,
tes grandes sœurs: Amour, Liberté, Poésie.

VIII

Il n'y avait que des troncs déchirés,
que couronnaient des vols de corbeaux ivres,
et le château était couvert de givre,
ce soir de fer où je m'y présentai.

Je n'avais plus avec moi ni mes livres,
ni ma compagne, l'âme, et ses péchés,
ni cette enfant qui tant rêvait de vivre
quand je l'avais sur terre rencontrée.

Les murs étaient blanchis au lait de sphinge
et les dalles rougies au sang d'Orphée.
Des mains sans grâce avaient tendu des linges

aux fenêtres borgnes comme des fées.
La scène était prête pour des acteurs
fous et cruels à force de bonheur.

VII

Drink down this cup of shades. Sleep, sleep, go down.
We'll take your wretchedness, borne like a crown,
to well-kept glades of death; and you then shaking
shall walk as one who dreams and walks unwaking:

slip through that door where no-one is allowed:
red windflowers fresh as night shall be your guide;
go out and pluck the myrtle golden-boughed
whose gleam shall lead you to the waterside

of the true life and pure accomplishment,
where thoughts are awesome, strong and confident.
Tomorrows will not end. Through dawns of blue,

healed spirit, they shall come to welcome you,
and hand in hand you'll know again your three
great sisters: Freedom, Love, and Poetry.

VIII

Only torn tree-trunks; drunken flight
of crows above them; that was all:
thick frost was on the fortress wall
when I walked in, that iron night.

I'd lost my books; the soul had gone,
my bosom friend, whose sins were rife;
I'd lost that girl who yearned for life
when we on earth stood one to one.

White sphinx's-milk ran down the walls;
red blood of Orpheus stained the flags;
at windows blind as wall-eyed trolls

crude hands had strung a screen of rags:
a stage for actors who enjoyed
being both cruel and paranoid.

IX

Traduit de Hugo von Hofmannsthal

Une coupe au bord de la bouche,
elle allait d'un si ferme pas
et la main si sûre que pas
une goutte ne se versa.

Il montait un cheval farouche.
Si sûre et ferme était sa main
que, frémissant au coup de frein,
le cheval s'arrêta soudain.

Et pourtant, quand la main légère
à l'autre main gantée de fer
cette simple coupe tendit,

ils tremblaient si fort, elle et lui,
que les mains ne se rencontrèrent,
et le vin noir se répandit.

(Toute lecture était interdite aux prisonniers. Un jour, pourtant, un fragment de la *Pariser Zeitung* me tomba sous la main. Mon compagnon de cellule et moi nous dévorâmes la feuille infâme: c'était tout de même quelque chose à lire. J'eus la joie d'y retrouver un sonnet de Hofmannsthal: *Die Beiden*, célèbre pièce d'anthologie qui m'avait toujours charmé et que, au cours d'une nuit d'insomnie, je m'efforçai d'adapter à notre langue.)

IX

Translated from Hugo von Hofmannsthal

Curved her lip, and curved the cup,
safely carried in her hand;
sure and easy was her tread,
not a single drop was shed.

Sure and steady was his hand,
and his horse high-spirited;
he with mastery pulled up,
made the startled creature stand.

Did the strong hand grasp the cup
that the fair one offered up?
It was not done easily.

How they trembled, he and she!
Hand by hand was never found,
and the dark wine stained the ground.

(The prisoners were forbidden anything to read. One day, though, a fragment of an issue of the *Pariser Zeitung* came into my hands. My cellmate and I devoured the evil print which was at any rate something to read. I had the joy of lighting on a sonnet of Hofmannsthal: *Die Beiden*, a famous piece from the anthologies which had always charmed me and which I adapted into our language by great efforts during one of my nights of insomnia).

X

Rose d'Alexandrie... C'était une chanson
qu'étoilaient et striaient les fusées de la plage.
Et la nuit éclatait de partout, comme à l'âge
où la première fête entre dans la maison.

Oui, une joie d'enfants nous pressait au balcon
d'où nous contemplions les danses du village.
Et pourtant, bien-aimée, que d'ombres sous ton front,
et que nos mains tremblaient en tournant cette page!

Mais dans l'été, c'était bien lui, dont brusquement
la griffe avait foncé sur nous, l'espoir dément!
Il était là – Il est peut-être là toujours.

Car nous sentons rôder le long de notre vie,
à travers la forêt où nos pas sont plus lourds,
une bête farouche et jamais assouvie.

XI

Compagne, tu n'auras connu de mon étoile
que la face nocturne et les yeux aveuglés
et cette bouche dure et tant d'aridité,
rien que l'abrupt aspect d'une ombre capitale.

Pour qui donc mes regards et les eaux musicales
que contenaient mes mains au temps de la clarté?
Mes promesses d'Asie se sont tôt écoulées
vers l'autre extrémité de la sphère fatale.

Retourne à ta lumière et penche-toi sur toi,
– car toi, ton ange ne cessait de croître, – et sois
une Narcisse sans orgeuil, désir ni larmes,

confuse et rougissant de se savoir trop belle.
Toi seule auras permis que j'offre à mes autels
une félicité faite à force d'alarmes.

X

Yes, 'Rose of Alexandria' was sung
as rockets streaked and starred along the shore:
the night was all lit up, as when the young
have carnival they never had before.

The balcony: our childish joy. Look down –
the villagers were dancing to the band.
We watched. And yet, my love, you wore a frown!
We turned this page with an unsteady hand.

But in the summer, there it was, the thing
that gripped and clawed us: moonstruck hankering!
Yes, there it was. Perhaps it never goes:

for through our lives we sense a prowling beast
across the forest, as our footfall slows –
malevolent, and not to be appeased.

XI

Companion: of my star you've only known
the midnight side, eyes that no longer see,
the granite mouth and the aridity,
capital shadow, cliff-face: this alone.

Who caught my eye, when waters, sweet to hear,
lay in my hands in that clear light of day?
My promises of Asia drained away
to the far limit of the fateful sphere.

Back to your light, be your own prop and stay
– your angel grew and grew – take pride away,
desire, and tears; with so much loveliness,

be a Narcissus, blushing and confused;
I'll offer up what you alone excused,
wrested from life's alarms: my happiness.

XII

Les songes assidus qui par la main se tiennent
et de tous mes parcours font un seul chemin noir
n'y soufflent une aussi dévastatrice haleine
que parce qu'en ton cœur, témoin de mon histoire,

je ne puis réfléchir qu'illusions et peines,
les astres languissants d'un errant promenoir,
une conjonction d'accords faux qui se traînent,
sans écho ni mesure, aux défauts des miroirs.

Si je m'abreuve de ton ciel, c'est que ton ciel
s'est empli jusqu'aux bords de ma coupe de fiel.
Mes yeux qu'en ton douloir mon douloir éblouit,

trous de flamme béants, alentour multiplient,
comme en la roue du paon autant de bleus ocelles,
tes regards déchirés aux rochers de ma nuit.

XIII

La rue monte jusqu'à la blanchisserie bleue
et découpe, déserte, un ciel de craie. Tu passes,
pèlerin des pavés livides et des places
où grelottent les bancs et les kiosques poudreux.

Quelle stupeur se peint où tu portes les yeux,
dans l'immobile cri des affiches, les glaces
figées des magasins naufragés et la face
de toutes ces maisons en attente du feu!

Va-t'en de ton chemin, sors de tous les chemins,
toi qui n'as pu jamais obtenir un destin!
C'est l'écho de tes pas qui forme un tel silence.

Mais que vitres et toits enfin vibrent de rire,
et les jardins des rois que ta seule présence,
sous le poids de sa cendre, empêche de surgir!

XII

The unrelenting thoughts that all link hands,
making my journeys one long dismal trail,
only blow such a breath of scything hail
because your heart, that sees each circumstance,

reflects my pain and error and mischance,
reflects my stars that stray and faint and fail,
a knot of discords and a dragging tail
without reflection, rhyme or resonance.

Your sky hurls rain on me: I let it fall.
Your sky brims over with my cup of gall.
My eyes are dazzled by our misery,

two yawning flame-pits. As a peacock's tail
teems with blue eyelets, my eyes multiply
your glances, which my crags of night impale.

XIII

Cutting a sky of chalk the steep road goes
to the blue laundry. Only you are there,
pilgrim of pallid cobbles, from some square
where benches creak and kiosks decompose.

Numb shock hangs painted where your eyes enquire:
the frozen cry of placards, the congealed
windows of clapped-out shops, the target-field
of housefronts waiting for the burst of fire!

Get off the road, get out of every road:
you never found that future you were owed!
Deep silence is the echo of your tread.

Let roofs and windows laugh in ecstasies,
let parks of kings shake off your presence dead,
beneath whose ashen weight they cannot rise!

XIV

Comme le sens caché d'une ronde enfantine,
qui n'a rêvé d'entendre un jour sa propre voix
et de voir son regard et de saisir le signe
que fait en s'éloignant la ligne de nos pas?

Ô mal aimée, le temps, cet imposteur insigne,
nous volait notre temps et s'envolait, narquois,
nous laissant un lambeau de sa chanson maligne
pour nous bercer. Pourtant il me semblait parfois

que cette vie n'était pas tout à fait la nôtre.
Mais non, vois-tu, c'était bien elle et non une autre.
La fille errante, aux mains brisées, venue s'asseoir,

un soir de vent, au coin de la cheminée froide,
mais regarde-la donc, regarde son regard
terrible d'oiseau triste et d'étoile malade.

XV

Lorsque nous entrerons dans cette ville chinoise,
je boiterai un peu, mais je connaîtrai l'amour.
Les pauvres fous, accroupis sous des charrues, aux bases
des murailles fiévreuses, des portes et des tours,

s'envoleront soudain pour nous guider aux citernes,
et une tiède lune, sœur de la fin du jour,
nous accueillera par son cortège de lanternes
et sa batterie de cymbales et de cris sourds.

J'irai, m'accrochant aux plis de ta robe chérie
et aux baisers furtifs de tes yeux de paradis,
de tes yeux de musique, de tes yeux de prière.

Oh! ce sera une récompense inattendue
que de découvrir, comme deux points d'astres perdus
et rallumés, le souffle de nos âmes légères.

XIV

The hidden meaning of a nursery rhyme:
to hear our own voice, really read our face:
this is our dream: and to decode, some time,
along the way, the line our footsteps trace.

My ill-beloved, that noted swindler, time,
stole all our time and slyly stole away,
leaving a sliver of his evil rhyme
to lull us. I kept feeling, anyway,

this life was not to all intents our own.
Ah, but it was, you see, and ours alone.
That drifter at our fire one windy night,

trying to warm her damaged hands – my word,
look at the look of her, an awful sight,
look of a blighted star, a suffering bird.

XV

When we pass through the Chinese city-gates
I'll stumble, but I'll be alive to love.
Poor souls, bent double under heavy weights,
with fevered walls and ports and towers above,

will lead us to the water-tanks, in haste.
A tepid moon, sister of dusk, will rise
to welcome us with lantern-trains, slow-paced,
with batteries of gongs and hollow cries.

I'll go, but cling to your dear dress's folds
and to the stealthy kisses of your eyes
of music, eyes of prayer and paradise.

Oh, it will be an unforeseen reward
to find again, like two star-points restored
from void to light, breath of our dancing souls.

XVI

Admoto occurrere fato (Lucain, IV, 480)

Viens, nous le trouverons au détour du chagrin,
au niveau de la nuit, à fleur de transparence.
Nous n'avons jusqu'ici connu que sa semblance,
mais à pas de voleur lui-même approche enfin.

Nous-mêmes qu'étions-nous sinon double silence,
couple d'ombres troublées d'unir de fausses mains?
Et nos mains, revêtues de vérité soudain,
béniront l'effrayant messager qui s'avance.

Il fait sombre. Il est tard. Mais que s'attarde encore
le noir épais de toute cette vie de mort!
Le reste ne fût-il qu'un fil de crépuscule,

un horizon de sang dans le calice amer
que devant notre soif l'ange en riant recule,
nous terrasserons l'ange et nous boirons la mer.

XVII

Éloignez-vous sur la pointe des pieds.
Prenez la barque et ne revenez plus.
Retournez tous chez vous avec vos fées,
vos ombres étrangères et vos luths.

Bien sûr, pour vous, beaux promeneurs, ce fut
une aventure neuve et enchantée.
Emportez-la comme un bijou volé,
un feu qui tremble encore, un livre lu.

C'est ici la chambre des anges morts.
Laissez-nous seuls dans notre vie déserte,
devant ces mains et ces ailes inertes.

Il s'est passé ici, depuis l'aurore,
une effrayante histoire, étrange et tendre,
et que le désespoir seul peut comprendre.

XVI

Admoto occurrere fato (Lucan, IV, 480)

Come, we shall find it at the pass of tears,
level with night, shallow as clarity.
We've only known its likeness. Stealthily,
sly as a thief, it finally appears.

We were a two-faced silence, shiftiness,
twin shadows joining hands, that told a lie:
hands we now turn, new-clothed with honesty,
to the grim messenger they soon will bless.

It's dark. It's late. But let's not expedite
this lifetime of the dead, this thick, black night!
And should the twilight leave the slightest trace,

a blood-horizon in the bitter cup
snatched by the grinning angel from our face,
we'll floor the angel, drink the ocean up.

XVII

Leave us on tiptoe, go away,
set sail and never come again:
go home, remove your fairy train,
your lutes, your foreign shadow-play.

Proud walkers, it was in your hand,
so take it, like a purloined ring,
a flame that flickers, tarrying,
a book you've read, a wonderland.

This is a room dead angels fill.
Our lives are arid. Leave us be,
where all these hands and wings lie still.

When day had dawned, this place could see
a tender, dreadful, strange affair,
understood only by despair.

XVIII

Celui qu'étoiles, vous avez pris comme cible
de vos cris anxieux et qu'allez pourchassant,
ne vous irritez plus s'il se rejette errant
aux bords du monde ardent et se fait invisible;

rien qu'un méchant fantôme, une ombre inaccessible
et pareille – vous rappelez-vous? – à l'Enfant
Prodigue de Rainer Maria s'enfuyant
pour ne pas être aimé de cet amour terrible.

Exigence des cœurs diffuse dans la nuit,
beaux regards confiants, détournez-vous de lui.
Et vous, mortes et morts, alourdis de pardons,

écartez votre vol de sa déserte grève.
Ah! c'est lui, cerf en pleurs, courbant enfin le front,
qui vient vous retrouver chaque soir dans ses rêves.

XIX

Je suis Jean (V. H.)

Je suis Jean. Je ne viens chargé d'aucun message.
Je n'ai rien vu dans l'île où je fus confiné,
rien crié au désert. Je porte témoignage
seulement pour le songe d'une nuit d'été.

Pour le songe d'une jeunesse retrouvée
sous les chaudes constellations d'un autre âge,
et parce que je veux entendre le langage
brûlant et vif de ce firmament éclaté.

Quant à moi, je ferai silence, étant indigne
de nouer le cordon des approches insignes
qui monteront vers l'aube ou d'apaiser mon front

sur le scintillement des hymnes révélées:
précurseur et disciple en toi s'aboliront,
ô nuit de l'ombre blanche et du total reflet!

XVIII

Stars, do not mind his going, since at him
you aimed your troubled shouts, your hue and cry.
Self-exiled, self-concealing, secretly
he wanders now at the enflamed world's rim,

a mere malignant ghost you cannot grasp.
Rainer Maria makes his Prodigal
Child run away just so, you may recall,
not to be cherished in that fearsome clasp.

Turn from him, friendly glances that confide,
heartfelt demands diffusing in the night.
And you, weighed down with pardons, you the dead,

cut out his barren sandbank from your flight.
He is the weeping stag that bows its head
and in its dreams comes nightly to your side.

XIX

I am John (V. H.)

I am John. I am not here for witnessing.
Imprisoned in the isle, I saw no sight;
I cried not in the wilderness. I bring
only the image of a summer night;

that is my message; and of youth, restored
in other times, a hot and starry sky.
I come to hear the burning, living word,
this shattered firmament's soliloquy.

I am unworthy (and shall hold my peace)
to tie the lace for that processional
climb to the bright dawn, salving ears and eyes

in the revealed and sparkling harmonies.
Precursor and disciple both shall cease
in you, white-shadowed night that mirrors all!

XX

À maison de feu ciel de pierre,
mais à ciel de pierre aile d'ange
bruissante en ripostes de fer.
Au clair de l'incessant échange,

c'est toi, le moindre souffle d'air,
langue légère, qui déranges
le diamant des vents contraires
et construis des règnes étranges.

Vive aurore se fasse airain,
ou roc le vaporeux de destin:
s'en rira l'inscrutable centre

d'où s'inspire un plus fier serpent.
Il neige. Et Noël, dans son antre,
couve quel métal étonnant?

XXI

Tombeau d'Antonio Machado

Âme sainte, la Charité,
guidant les saintes de la nuit,
aborde aux lieux déshonorés
que ta torche en vain purifie.

Elles vont délivrer tes cendres
d'un pays qui n'est plus que sable
et, vol d'oiseaux clairs, les répandre
à travers un ciel respirable.

Là tu trouveras l'odeur
de tes profonds étés en pleurs.
Il ne restera plus jamais

qu'une urne brisée de colère,
à Collioure, au pied des pierres
où pourrissent les prisonniers.

XX

Stony sky to household flare;
but in loud and sharp exchange,
angel's wing of ironware.
Lit by endless interchange,

you, the slightest breath of air,
you, light tongue, shall disarrange
stormwinds' diamond solitaire
and assemble kingdoms strange.

Glowing dawn may turn to brass;
rock, the future's swirling gas:
and the hidden heart shall then

laugh, a serpent's pride to raise.
Snow. Will Christmas in its den
hatch some metal to amaze?

XXI

Tomb of Antonio Machado

Saintly heart, Love's spirit flies,
guiding night's angelic band
near the scenes of infamy
your light cannot purify.

From a country turned to sand
they shall bring your noble dust,
bright birds, flying. This they cast
on the living, breathing skies.

Yours again, the fragrancy
of your summers' poignancy.
Nothing shall survive and stay

but an urn, smashed angrily
near Collioure's masonry
where the jailbait rots away.

XXII

En tous pays, depuis toujours, les ouvriers
meurent. Le sang des ouvriers baigne les rues.
Les ouvriers crient et tombent dans la fumée.
Le feu, le froid, la faim, le fer et la roue tuent

les ouvriers. En tous pays de pierres nues,
d'abres pourris, de grilles d'hospices rouillées,
depuis toujours, par la misère des journées,
le troupeau des journées saignées et abattues…

Ô Dieu de justice qui régnez, non aux cieux,
mais dans le cœur de l'homme, au cœur de sa colère,
ne vous répandrez-vous donc jamais sur la terre?

Seigneur des forts et de la force, ouvrez les yeux!
Les bouches sont muettes, les poings sont liés,
et la chaîne est très longue. Mais les ouvriers?

XXIII

La plaie que, depuis le temps des cerises,
je garde en mon cœur s'ouvre chaque jour.
En vain les lilas, les soleils, les brises
viennent caresser les murs des faubourgs.

Pays des toits bleus et des chansons grises,
qui saignes sans cesse en robe d'amour,
explique pourquoi ma vie s'est éprise
du sanglot rouillé de tes vieilles cours.

Aux fées rencontrées le long du chemin
je vais racontant Fantine et Cosette.
L'arbre de l'école, à son tour, répète

une belle histoire où l'on dit: demain …
Ah! jaillisse enfin le matin de fête
où sur les fusils s'abattront les poings!

XXII

The workers in all lands eternally
die. Workers' blood goes streaming underfoot.
The workers stumble in the smoke; they cry.
Fire, winter, iron, the wheel, and hunger put

the workers down. In all lands rotting trees,
bare stones, the rusty grilles of hospices,
since time began, the days of wretchedness,
the herd of days bloodied and on their knees...

O God of justice, throned not in the skies,
but in the heart of man, and of his wrath,
will you not spread your wings at last on earth?

Lord of the strong, of force, unveil your eyes!
The wrists are tied, the lips speak not a word,
the chain is very long. The workers, Lord?

XXIII

Since cherry-time I've nursed, deep down,
a wound that opens every day,
while by the walls of Anytown
lilacs and suns and breezes play.

Land of blue roofs and grey refrains
that bleeds in love's romantic dress,
tell me why each old yard enchains
my life with tears and rustiness.

I teach the pixies on my way
all about Smike and Little Nell.
In time the playground tree will tell

a rousing tale: one day, one day ...
Stream forth, bright dawn of carnival,
when fists have guns to spark the fray!

XXIV

Briques et tuiles, etc. (Verlaine)

Plomb, zinc et fer,
ô les charmants
petits enfers
pour les amants!

Mer et désert:
l'événement
n'a rien à faire
pour le moment.

À tous nos coups
le néant joue
échec et mat.

L'histoire close
plus jamais n'ose
produire un Acte.

XXV

Paris, ses monuments de sang drapés, son ciel
couleur aile d'avion, dans le soleil couchant,
j'ai tout revu, et j'entendais renaître un chant
lointain, pareil à une levée d'étincelles.

J'ai si longtemps aimé, il y a si longtemps,
cette ville dans une chambre aux murs de miel
et d'aube vieille, au plafond bas. Et dans le gel
du miroir pâle un fier visage méditant.

Et les meubles étaient d'acajou. Sur le marbre
une flûte. Par la vitre plombée, les arbres
– des marronniers – dessinaient leur feuillé, très vert.

Je sais: j'étais debout, près de cette fenêtre,
et les pavés retentissaient d'un bruit de fête,
une fête de tous les jours, comme la mer.

XXIV

Briques et tuiles, etc. (Verlaine)

Lead, iron and tin,
snug sulphur-mines
for Valentines
to sizzle in!

Ocean and sand:
the great event
is impotent
as matters stand.

All that we do
the void has checked,
checkmated too.

The final page
has no Effect
that it can stage.

XXV

Paris, her blood-draped monuments, her sky
at sundown, aircraft-grey: all this again
I've seen, and heard a faraway refrain
coming to new birth, like the sparks that fly.

Paris, so long my love, so long ago,
inside a room, low-ceilinged, walls the shade
of honey and old dawn: pale frost displayed
my proud and pensive face, a mirror-show.

The furniture, mahogany; glass stood
on marble. Through the leaded light, the wood
and greenleaf pattern of a chestnut-tree.

I know: I stood beside that window, there.
The cobbles threw back noises of a fair,
a fair as plain and simple as the sea.

XXVI

À peine si le cœur vous a considérées,
        images et figures
que la succession des concerts fait durer
        plus que tout ce qui dure,

ô mes belles amours, dont les pays dorés
        reflètent la peinture,
et déjà les adieux qui vont nous séparer
        s'égalent à vos pures

éternités. Oui, ce sera l'unique fois
que, s'étranglant, nos voix loueront enfin vos voix
        de ne jamais se taire.

Va, brise-toi joyeusement, cœur désolé,
car le plus démuni des mortels meurt comblé
        d'avoir aimé la terre.

XXVII

Ami, s'il ne fait pas assez noir dans ta nuit,
c'est que, je ne sais où, ton beau château s'apprête
à célébrer pour toi quelque étonnante fête
dont un éclat déjà glisse jusqu'à ton lit.

Un empire inconnu de pompe et de conquête,
comme un bond dans le creux des ténèbres tapi,
c'est lui qui te contraint à vouloir plus parfaite
l'ombre où ton encre et tes rideaux lourds s'ingénient.

Coupe de lait obscur percée de traits solaires,
toute offrande à la mort retourne à la lumière,
et la fleur des secrets expire en fruit de foudre.

Tu le sais, favori des visites d'hiver,
et que c'est au plus dur du mur de fer que s'ouvrent,
comme en des chairs blessées, les portes de la mer.

XXVI

The heart has scarcely pondered you at all,
        figures and images,
that every confluence makes durable
        beyond whatever is,

my splendid loves, whose golden native lands
        reflect the painter's art;
already we prefigure, with these hands
        that must unclasp and part,

your pure eternities. Yes, now alone,
our stifled voices shall acclaim your own
        unconquerable voice.

Go, grieving heart, be shattered, and rejoice:
the most bereft die loving in full measure
        this earth we treasure.

XXVII

Friend, if you need more blackness in your night,
your stately pile is plotting, who knows where,
a special gathering for your delight:
your bed's already fingered by the glare.

Conquest and pomp, unheard-of tyranny,
a crouching leap into the dismal pit,
make you seek out a deeper ebony,
thick drapes, a blacker ink to hone your wit.

Cup of dark milk pierced by a solar ray,
what's offered up to death regains the day;
shy blooms expire, the fruit's a thunderball.

You know it, darling of the winter's call,
and that the sea's gates open and make way,
like flesh-wounds, at the hardest iron wall.

XXVIII

Ce seul plaisir nourrit mes heures solitaires,
de redire à mon cœur que je sais ce qui fut.
Je mets ma certitude en des romans confus
et peuple de destins un continent polaire.

Je répète qu'un soir une jeune chimère
fit résonner la corde amoureuse du luth
perdu sur la table de l'auberge. Et j'ai vu
le voyageur traînet son secret sur la terre.

Après tant de hasards un prisonnier qui meurt
entend comme un adieu la chanson du pêcheur
dans le soleil du golfe. Et il y eut, profonde

amie, ô fantaisie, ces chers et brefs moments.
La vie s'est refermée sur quelques purs amants.
Une main a passé sur la face du monde.

XXIX

Habilleuse des morts, fais naître une princesse
de cette morte nue comme un galet des flots.
Suscite sous tes doigts les plus riches caresses
qui jamais aient surpris la moelle de ses os.

Que palpite la nuit dans le bleu de ses tresses
et que la lune en feu découvre ses yeux clos.
Verse un émail de neige dans ses seins et presse
ses bras vides sous de splendides oripeaux.

Je la vois désormais assise dans l'espace,
élevant une fleur à hauteur de ma face,
ou marcher d'un pas dur comme sur des remparts,

heureuse, oh! bienheureuse, et de traîner si fière
la flûte et le tambour fascinés des regards
dans le satin de son frisson vif, ma vipère.

XXVIII

One pleasure feeds my lonely hours: to tell
my heart again, I know what used to be.
I fill an Arctic waste with puppetry,
putting my truths in books not written well.

A young chimera made the love-chord sound
one evening on the lute – this I declare –
lost on the tavern table. I saw, there,
the traveller trail his secret on the ground.

A captive whose ninth life is sputtering
hears, as a farewell, fishermen who sing
across the sunlit gulf. Yes, let's pretend!

We had those dear brief times, my deepest friend.
Life closed back in on some pure souls who loved;
across the wide world's face a hand has moved.

XXIX

Dresser of corpses, conjure a princess
from this poor corpse as bare as pebblestones.
Rouse with your touch a worthier caress
than ever shook the marrow of her bones.

Let night pulse in her hair's blue loveliness
and fiery moon unveil her lidded eyes.
Pour snow's enamel in her breasts, and press
her empty arms with splendid trumperies.

From this day on I see her, throned in space,
holding a flower up about my face,
or marching smartly like a sentinel,

happy, so happy, and so proud to take
the fife and drum, enraptured by her spell,
in her quick shudder's silk, my viper-snake.

XXX

Squelette d'or au long des murailles scellées,
le dormeur éveillé promène sa misère
victorieuse et le trésor émerveillé
d'une ingénuité indulgente aux chimères,

et vous, fontaines obstinées des cimetières,
gorges des rossignols, ô ruisselants métiers,
cordes dans le matin, marteaux, roues dentelées,
cris, fleurs, cercueils, moulins à pains ou à prières ...

Et le scribe est heureux, et la plume est heureuse,
et l'arpenteur, le peintre, et la main rigoureuse,
et l'œil numérateur, et les splendeurs des jours

égales aux splendeurs que racontent les nuits.
Adorés nonchalants, passez! Cueillez nos fruits!
Ravissez nos raisins et nos pommes d'amour!

XXXI

Qu'il soit au moins permis à cette lyre obscure,
consternée sous la croix brouillée des galeries,
de relever, dans un éclair, sa voix meurtrie
et de t'apercevoir, bel athlète futur.

Glaive sur l'escalier des monstres assoupis!
Père du long matin, fils de la pourriture,
c'est toi qui briseras les os et les jointures
de ce double accroché comme une maladie

à des corps déjà lourds à traîner dans les veilles,
mais désormais joyeux de vomir le sommeil.
Les yeux ne voudront plus dormir. Midi sans trêve

arrachera leur ombre aux pieds des messagers.
Oh! ce soir soit pour nous le dernier soir tombé,
et puisqu'il faut rêver, rêvons la mort des rêves.

XXX

Gold-skeletoned, by walls of fortresses
the one who slept parades his misery
triumphant, and the wide-eyed treasury
of tricks that put chimeras at their ease.

You graveyard fountainheads, persistent springs,
nightingales' throats and rivulets of skills,
cords in the morning, cogwheels, hammerings,
cries, flowers, coffins, breadmills, prayermills ...

The penman and the pen have their good hour;
joy comes to those who paint and who survey;
sure hand, appraising eye; the glorious day

matching the fabled glories of the night.
Come, carefree sweethearts! Pluck our fruits, devour
our grapes and golden apples of delight!

XXXI

Grant that this lyre in its obscurity,
stunned by the addled cross of galleries,
may raise its bruised voice to the lightning skies,
and see the handsome athlete you shall be.

Sword on the stairs of monsters comatose!
Long morning's father, putrefaction's son,
disjoint and break the doubled shank of bone
that battens, like a sickness, on all those

bodies too gross for the long haul of night,
who now disgorge their slumber, with delight.
Eyes shall reject sleep, runners' feet lose all

their shade: no mercy from the noonday sky.
Let us now see no further evenings fall:
since we must dream, let's dream that dreams must die.

XXXII

L'univers insulté peut tenir sa vengeance,
les jours renaître au jour et les soirs consolés
répandre leur rosée de sang et d'innocence
et s'ouvrir à la nuit comme des mains lavées.

Revanche dans le ciel, totale et sans clémence!
Oui, le tonnerre peut soulager la forêt.
Mais toi, tu n'obtiendras pour toi que le silence
qui suit l'effacement de la chose jugée:

Le blanc silence aux ailes de neige éperdues,
dont le cri forcené mesure l'étendue
        de l'assouvissement suprême.

Au point où le mépris toute digue a rompue,
cœur près de se briser, il ne te reste plus
        qu'à mépriser le mépris même.

XXXIII

Quel est ton nom? – Constance. – Où vas-tu? – Je m'en viens
de toi-même et retourne à toi-même. – Soulève
ce linceul de ta face, et que je sache au moins
si tu ressembles à la sœur d'un de mes rêves.

– Il n'est pas temps encore. – Ainsi je ne puis rien
sur toi? – Silence! Apprends que je suis ta captive
et qu'à chacun des coups soufferts par ton destin
se forme un trait de plus à ma beauté furtive.

Lorsque sera parfait ce visage fidèle,
ton cœur y pourra lire, aux lueurs de ton ciel,
et tes choix accomplis et tes maux acceptés.

Brèves sont tes amours. Comptées et déjà mortes.
Mais ce sont tes amours. Et ta mort, tu l'emportes
toute avec toi. Persiste, et tu seras sauvé.

XXXII

The outraged universe stores up redress;
days are reborn at daybreak; dusk's half-light,
consoled, distils its blood and gentleness,
and opens like washed hands towards the night.

Vengeance in heaven: total, no remorse!
Yes, thunder soothes the fevered trees, no doubt;
when you are judged, that silence shall be yours,
the silence when the judged are blotted out:

white silence, snowy wings, abandonment,
whose frenzied cry marks out the true extent
        of the supreme excessiveness.

When hate and scorn have shattered every wall,
heart close to breaking, what remains at all
        but to hate hate, scorn scorn, no less?

XXXIII

'Your name is – ?' 'Constancy.' – 'Your course?' – 'I flow
from you and back to you.' 'Your face, it seems,
is shrouded. Let me see it, and I'll know
if you are like the sister in my dreams.'

'Too soon.' 'Then I am yours, and powerless?'
'Silence. Hear this. I am your captive pawn;
each of the fateful blows that you have borne
has added to my hidden loveliness.

This face shall reach perfection, true and right:
your heart shall read there, by your heaven's light,
each choice you made, each evil done to you.

Your loves are brief; already counted; cold.
Yet they are yours. Your death you have, and hold,
and carry off. Endure, and so win through.'

Poems from

THE ROSE AND THE WINE

LA ROSE ET LE VIN

A rose that was drowning
in wine in a bowl,
all loosened and swooning,
breathed out life and soul.

*

Une rose s'est noyée
dans une coupe de vin,
et, défaillante, effeuillée,
elle exhale son destin.

The following poems have been extracted from a sequence of 31 poems and prose poems (with commentaries) entitled *The Rose & the Wine.* The roman numeral at the foot of the page / poem indicates each poem's position in the original sequence.

L'ÉLÉMENT

L'élément et la créature
s'aiment étrangement d'amour.
Ce qui se prolonge et qui dure
s'éprend de la danse des jours.

Dur de lumière et de silence,
le sel du monde s'attendrit
en ondes de magnificence
dans le feu du soupir des nuits.

Un prince égaré sous l'orage
rencontre au détour des forêts
une mendiante suavage
dont il reste transverbéré.

COMMENTAIRE

«L'éternité est amoureuse des productions du temps.» (William Blake.)

Le Vin est l'élément, la Rose est la créature. Voilà ce qu'ils sont devenus tous deux, le Vin et la Rose, lui l'élément, ce qui se rapproche le plus de l'énormité massive, opaque, de l'éternité, et elle, la Rose, une création de notre humaine durée. C'est par l'élément, forme involuée de l'éternité, que celle-ci peut exprimer son hurlant amour de la petite – merveilleuse – beauté d'ici-bas.

... Bah! toutes deux, en somme, la Rose et le Vin, productions du temps, épanouies et fragiles sous le regard amoureux de l'éternité absente, absorbée, évanouie. Le prince est l'élément; la mendiante sauvage, c'est la pauvre créature sublime.

(XVI)

ELEMENT AND CREATURE

Element and creature have,
Curiously, a mutual love.
That which self-prolongs and stays
falls in love with dance of days.

Hard with silence and with light,
salt of the world is turning tender,
softens into waves of splendour
in the fire of sighs of night.

Lost in storms, a monarch's child
in the forest's winding ways
meets a beggar-woman wild
and is smitten all his days.

COMMENTARY

'Eternity is in love with the productions of time.' (William Blake.)

The Wine is the element, the Rose is the creature. Here is what they have both become, the Wine and the Rose: he (the Wine) is the element, that which most nearly approaches the massive, opaque vastness of eternity, and she, the Rose, a creation of our human time-span. It is through the element, an involuted form of eternity, that she can express her howling love of the miniature, marvellous beauty that is ours, here below.

... The answer is that both the Rose and the Wine are productions of time, spreading and fragile under the amorous gaze of absent, absorbed, vanished eternity. The prince is the element; the wild beggar-woman is the poor sublime creature.

(XVI)

DÉLIRANTE D'AMOUR

Délirante d'amour à cause des ombreuses
et nocturnes idées
qui, lucioles bleues et promeneuses follcs,
son errance guidaient,

cime, chef de la rose, ivresse somnambule,
ouverte à la fraîcheur
des soirs perdus dans les sonores vestibules
du ciel intérieur,

enfant volée de la folie, enfant voleuse
en robe de bonheur
accrochée aux chemins rapides des rieuses
églantines en fleur,

lune aux pas de la lune et nulle part lassée
d'un si trouble parcours
dans les jardins déments par quelle main tracé
au nom de quel amour,

quel crime dans sa griffe éparse l'a saisie
et la tient balancée,
pensée, pensée, pensée, hagarde rêverie,
mourante renversée?

AMOUR D'AMOUR

Amour d'amour l'a prise dans ses lacs,
amour sans fin d'amour la sollicite,
chute sans fond et prison sans limite,
deuil sans raison et peine sans soulas.
Il n'est soleil ni lune à sa journée,
rien ne peut plus faire objet à ses pas,
ni ne peut mort être sa destinée.

(vi & viii)

DELIRIOUS WITH LOVE

Delirious with love in the toils of ideas
        of night and of shade,
blue fireflies and vagabond will-of-the-wisps
        her guides as she strayed,

highest tip of the rose, drunken sleepwalking joy,
        to the breeze opened wide
of evenings mislaid in the echoing halls
        of the heaven inside,

child lifted from folly, a light-fingered child
        wearing joy for a gown,
that clings to quick pathways of bright eglantines,
        laughing roses full-blown,

moon in step with the moon and unwearied by all
        the wild ways she must rove
in the light-headed gardens: ways, traced by what hand
        in the name of what love:

what crime has her gripped in its wide bony claw
        and holds her suspended,
the thought, thought, thought and the haggard-faced dream,
        to be dying, upended?

LOVE OF LOVE

Love of love caught her in its toils,
love without end of love embroils her,
bottomless fall and limitless prison,
pain without solace, grief without reason.
No sun nor moon makes bright her day,
nothing can stand across her path,
nor can death be her destiny.

(VI & VIII)

CRUCIFIÉE SUR DEUX BRANCHES

Crucifiée sur deux branches de sang,
étroite étoile à la tête qui penche,
oh! si docile à l'immobile instant,
charme blessé, chaste épouse, elle sent
l'ombre et la mort qui de ses mains s'épanchent.

Les pleurs s'en vont, les pleurs épanouis
trop lourds pour elle. Et ses oiseaux la quittent.
Elle les voit de leurs ailes meurtries
s'arracher vers un espace inouï.
Puis son regard même la déshabite.

Ne restait plus dans sa gorge oppressée,
liquide voix à pleurer souveraine,
qu'un long silence aux gerbes de rosée
qui retombaient dans les nuits cadencées.
Et le silence est mort à perdre haleine.

NE ME REGARDEZ PAS

Ne me regardez pas avec ces yeux d'extase:
vous ne sauriez, Marie, détourner mon regard.
Je contemple et je plains, sous le faix qui l'écrase,
Marthe, votre humble sœur, assise dans le noir.

Elle a trouvé son ciel sous les cendres frileuses.
Ne cherchez pas le vôtre aux pâleurs de mon front.
Ne me retenez pas dans vos mains lumineuses,
mais laissez-moi baiser l'ombre de sa maison.

Laissez-moi m'approcher de ce voile qui traîne
au bord de son labeur comme un soupir du soir.
Marie, Marie, de quoi vous mettez-vous en peine?
        Marthe a pris la meilleure part.

(v & xvii)

ON TWO BLOOD-BRANCHES

On two blood-branches like the Rood,
the narrow star whose head hangs low
as time stands still, so meek, so good,
chaste wife and wounded charm, must know
that death and dark from her hands flow.

Too great a load, her tears have gone,
her spreading tears. Her birds have fled.
She sees them speed on buffeted
bruised wings towards a space unknown.
Then her own gaze vacates, goes dead.

In stifled throat it only leaves,
where liquid voice had power to weep,
long silence of the dewy sheaves
that lapsed in rhythmic nights to sleep.
And silence chokes, and death relieves.

DON'T LOOK AT ME

Don't look at me with those ecstatic eyes,
Mary, you cannot hope to turn my head.
I see your sister's chores, and sympathise:
Martha sits meekly where the shadows spread.

She's found her heaven in the ashes cold:
Don't think to find yours on my pallid brows.
Free me of your bright hands, release your hold,
and let me kiss the shadow of her house.

Let me approach this veil, this sigh of eve,
dragged at the edges of her drudgery.
Oh Mary, Mary, you've no cause to grieve:
she took the better part, you see.

(v & xvii)

TAIS-TOI

Tais-toi, c'est une déchirure en moi qui brûle
quand je te vois, plus tard et seule, au crépuscule,
t'enfoncer dans les rues des ultimes cités.
Ce sera l'hiver du monde. L'air déserté
ne reconnaîtra plus ton souffle, petite âme.
Dans tes cheveux raidis d'astres givrés la flamme
des parfums d'autrefois ne s'allumera plus.
Tu pleureras le long des quais où les élus
élèvent leurs maisons comme des forteresses
ivres d'ailes en fleur et battant d'allégresse.
Et toi, sous ton fichu, dans leurs vitres, pâleur
spectrale, tu feras peur à ta propre peur.
Oh! tu voudras, tout bas, m'adresser des paroles
comme font, dans le vent, les bouvières folles,
et tes pas se perdront dans les pas des chômeurs,
des servantes chassées, des amers inventeurs,
de tous ceux qui s'en vont traînant aux carrefours
quelque chose comme un enfant malade et lourd.
Certes je n'ai moi-même jamais su bien faire
ce qu'il fallait avec les êtres de la terre,
et tout était trop difficile, affreusement ...
Mais, partage adoré, voilà que maintenant
tu ne te réfugieras plus dans ma faiblesse,
et le juste soleil d'été, à ta détresse
n'attachera qu'une ombre, une ombre, seule et si
mince elle-même et chaque jour plus amincie!
Tu n'auras plus qu'un nom, qu'une voix, qu'un malheur.
Ton cœur, ô mon cher cœur, ne sera que ton cœur,
et mon absence ton désert, et toi perdue,
oh! quand je pense à toi perdue, je ne veux plus
mourir! Je ne veux plus mourir, rose des roses!
Et je crie au destin: *Il est donc une chose*
que j'aime désormais plus que ma mort.
Ô toi,
cœur palpitant, beauté menacée dans mes bras,
horizon de mes yeux par toi, mes yeux, ô vie,
ma vie, enfant trouvée, retrouvée dans un cri
par ce retour de tes beaux yeux chaque matin,
j'atteste, je réponds, j'appelle, je maintiens ...

(XXI)

HUSH NOW

Hush now, for there's a wound in me that burns,
seeing you, all alone as night returns,
plunge into streets of cities all remote.
In the world's winter, soul, your breath shall not
be recognised by the deserted air.
The frozen stars shall stiffen all your hair,
your former perfumes shall not spark the blaze.
You'll weep on quaysides where the chosen raise
mansions like fortresses, whose drunken wings
burst into flower with joyous flutterings.
You'll be a pallid ghost behind your lace,
give your own fright a fright, a mirrored face.
You'll want to murmur to me, I suppose,
like barmy cattlewomen when it blows;
you'll merge your footsteps with the workless poor,
bitter inventors, skivvies shown the door,
and all who drag through crossroads of the town
something that, like a sick child, weighs them down.
For sure I've never had the competence
to do what's right by earth's inhabitants:
all was too difficult, extremely so ...
but, my own part and parcel, there you go:
you won't retreat into my feebleness;
the summer sun, requiting your distress,
will fix on it one shadow, only one,
so slim, and slimmer as the days go on.
You'll only have a name, a voice, a hurt.
Your heart, dear heart, will only be your heart;
my absence, your waste land. The loss of you!
Thinking you lost, I lose the will to die!
O rose of roses, no more will to die!
From this day on, I call to Destiny,
I love one thing above my death.
O you,
beating heart, threatened beauty I embrace,
my eyes' horizon, o you life, my eyes,
my life, child found and found again in cries
at each new day's return of your dear eyes,
I plead, appeal, bear witness, state my case ...

(XXI)

VIN QUI BÉNIS

Vin qui bénis le soir de l'ouvrier,
vin qui remplis l'âme de l'ivrognesse,
vin de poussière au poing du charretier,
vin de l'injure où grince la tendresse,
vin qui bénis le soir de l'ouvrier!

Vin de la table et de la tache bleue,
vins des chemins aux rencontres étranges,
vin des chemins aux soudains coups de feu,
vin des chemins où cheminent les anges,
vin de la table et de la tache bleue!

Vin des chemins, des rouliers, des sorcières,
vin de lucarne close au vagabond,
vin du coq noir à la gorge de pierre,
vin des forêts en des pays sans fond,
vin de chemins, des rouliers, des sorcières!

Vin des pays naufragés, vin des flots,
vin des baisers parjurés, vin des lâches,
vin du remords qui remonte sur l'eau,
vin du dégoût qu'on rabâche et qu'on crache,
vin des pays naufragés, vin des flots!

Vin des flots bleus qui tournent en rengaine,
vin âcre, vin vomi des mauvais soirs,
vin des couteaux étincelants de haine,
vin des pendus au ciel du désespoir,
vin des flots bleus qui tournent en rengaine!

Vin va-nu-pieds, vin mort de faim, vin rouge,
vin rouge bord, rouge mort, rouge feu,
vin bourdonnant aux ténèbres des bouges,
vin rougeoyant aux cavernes des gueux,
vin va-nu-pieds, vin mort de faim, vin rouge!

Vin qu'il faut boire enfin et boire encore,
comme le sang aux gorges des colombes,

WINE, THAT BLESSES

Wine, that blesses the worker's night,
wine of the dust in the drayman's grasp,
wine of the lush when her heart is light,
wine of the insult's delicate rasp,
wine, that blesses the worker's night!

Wine of the table and two blue spots,
wine of the roads of the strange exchange,
wine of the roads of the sudden shots,
wine of the roads where the angels range,
wine of the table and two blue spots!

Wine of the road and the woman-wizard,
wine of the deep-down dells, and the drover,
wine of the black rooster's stony gizzard,
wine of the skylight shut against a rover,
wine of the roads and the woman-wizard!

Wine of the shipwrecked lands and the tides,
wine of false kisses and gutless rabble,
wine of remorse, and the waves it rides,
wine of disgust that we dribble and gabble,
wine of the shipwrecked lands and the tides!

Wine of blue waves of the tired old tales,
wine of the hate that the knives shine by,
sour wine spewed on the night that fails,
wine of the hanged on a hopeless sky,
wine of blue waves of the tired old tales!

Wine going barefoot, starving, red,
wine that buzzes in the dark dug-out,
red for the brink, for the fire, for the dead,
ruddy in the dens of the down-and-out,
wine going barefoot, starving, red!

Wine to be drained and be drained again,
wine like the blood in the throat of a dove,

comme un poison strié de météores,
jusqu'à la lie aux épaisseurs de tombe,
vin qu'il faut boire enfin et boire encore

avec ce poids de tombe qui retombe.

(XXVII)

ET LA LUMIÈRE FUT

Et la lumière fut, qui éclaire tout homme
en ce monde et toute la misère du monde,
et qui forme l'éclat des raisins et des pommes
et les jaunes frissons sous les feuilles profondes.

Et la lumière est pure alors qu'elle arrondit
ses touches de splendeur sur la masse des ombres,
comme une lampe aimée que la main de la nuit
plonge au fond de l'amour par un escalier sombre.

Et la lumière est pure et la lumière est sainte,
et la lumière parle avec des mots joyeux
plus haut que la tempête et plus fort que la plainte
qui réveille en sursaut les dormeurs malheureux.

Sois louée, sois bénie, lumière inexhaustible,
thyrse de poésie, serpent de guérison,
peine et joie consenties, immanence visible,
conscience casquée, ô déesse raison!

Sois bénie, et béni soit ton règne efficace:
qu'il étende ses bras de révélation
comme des nappes d'or au large des espaces
et y fasse tinter les tours bleues des Sions.

Manifeste les sons étreints par le silence,
délivre les pitiés, les charmes engourdis:
il est encor des poids pour la juste balance,
il est encor des pleurs qui n'ont pas été dits.

wine like a meteor's poison-vein,
down to the dregs in the thick thick grave,
wine to be drained and be drained again,

tomb-tumbling, gravity down to the grave.

(XXVII)

AND THERE WAS LIGHT

And there was light, that lightens everyone
that lives, and lightens all this world's distress,
puts bloom on grapes and apples in the sun,
under low leaves a shivering yellowness.

The light is pure when it rounds out its glory
on fields of shadow touched with splendour bright,
a well-loved lamp to reach an upper storey,
thrust into Love's depths by the hand of night.

The light is pure, the light has sanctity,
and the light speaks, its words rejoice the heart,
above the storm and moaning threnody
that wakes unhappy sleepers with a start.

Be praised, be blessed, light inexhaustible,
serpent of healing, poets' thyrsus, yes,
pain and joy sanctioned, immanence visible,
goddess of reason, helmeted consciousness!

Blessings be on you and your potent reign:
may it stretch forth its arm, enlightening,
like cloth of gold spread wide across the plain,
and make the high blue towers of Sions ring.

Show forth the sounds that were constrained in silence:
set pity free, shake loose the magic word;
there are yet makeweights for the rightful balance,
there are yet tears whose story is unheard.

Des abîmes de deuil et de mémoires vaines
attendent ton signal, et d'obscurs continents
fumant, sur leurs degrés, d'odeurs suburréennes,
et des clairons muets au seuil des monuments.

Ta suscitation doit faire comparaître
toutes ces draperies grouillantes, mille espoirs,
poings convulsés aux grilles rouges des fenêtres,
comme une tragédie fermée de toutes parts.

Éclaire de tes yeux la minutie des rides,
la multiplicité des plis, la belle trace
des vagues accouplées et des cheveux rapides
que dénombre le vent aux profils qui s'effacent.

Exalte les vallées où les peuples gémissent,
couchés sur les tombeaux des âges embaumés,
fends les temples, pénètre au secret des calices
où bourdonne l'essaim des anges oubliés.

Prends les rues dans tes rais comme des ronces. Mêle
à tes fruits irisés les bulles des ruisseaux,
la paille des fumiers, le cri des étincelles
farouche et sans répit sous le choc des marteaux.

Ouvre les portes! L'âme est noire dans son coin,
et cette odeur de sang qui brûle plaît aux mères.
Mais tu sais rire, et d'un rire chaste et sans fin,
jusque parmi les fleurs pourries des cimetières,

toi, tu sais rire, et comme d'un rire espagnol,
torrent de flamme et d'eau sauvage, ma lumière,
mon grand sarcasme phrygien, ma carmagnole,
cheval, cheval terrible, ô la plus libre et fière

des apparitions au-dessus de nos têtes!
Tue les dieux mauvais, tue! Oh! quel dégoût croupit
dans nos siècles comme des restes de planètes
retombés loin de toi dans l'éternelle nuit!

Chasms of mourning and vain memories
await your signal; murky continents,
steaming with old Suburan fragrances;
mute bugles on the steps of monuments.

At your arousal, everything appears:
the thousand hopes, the vermin-ridden drapes,
the fists convulsing at red window-bars,
a tragedy that nobody escapes.

Illumine with your eyes the waves in pairs,
the plethora of folds, the lovely trace
of wrinkled intricacies, and quick hairs,
counted by winds, on brows the years efface.

The peoples cry aloud. Exalt the valleys!
They lie on centuries entombed in balm.
Cleave, cleave the temples, penetrate the chalice
where the forgotten angels buzz and swarm.

Embrace roads in your rays like briars. Bring,
mingled with rainbow fruits, the rivers' bubbles,
straw of the dunghills, sparks that fiercely sing,
relentless, as the hammer-blow redoubles.

Open the gates! The soul is black, unseen;
this is the burnt-blood smell a mother craves.
But you laugh well: your laugh is endless, clean,
even to the flowers that wither on the graves.

Yes, you laugh well, my light, à l'éspagnole,
flame and wild cataract, a streaming flood,
my Phrygian caustic wit, my carmagnole,
terrible steed, the freest and most proud

of airy apparitions. Kill, oh kill
the wicked gods! As dregs of planets fall,
our aeons of disgust are festering still,
crashed far from you in night perpetual.

Mais ne nous quitte pas! Embrase jusqu'à l'or
la plaie qui nous dévore et ces choses petites
et innocentes, nées à peine dans la mort,
la pauvre mort chétive et elle aussi bénite,

la misérable mort d'ici, notre seul bien,
(et c'est pourquoi tu sais que nous l'aimions ...). Mais d'autres
amours nous captiveront que ce triste rien,
quand tout n'appartiendra plus qu'à ta flamme haute,

porté vers cette épée ascensionnelle. Et tout
sera clair et présent. Radieuse, la terre
aura vêtu sa robe virginale d'août
pour boire infiniment le vin de la lumière.

(XXIX)

But stay amongst us! Burn to glowing gold
the wound that feasts on us, the littleness,
things small and innocent and scarcely foaled
before they die the death we also bless;

death's all we have on earth, and that is why
you know we loved it ... Many a better love
will charm us than that dismal nullity,
when all reverts to your high flame above,

nearing the sword of the ascension. All
shall then be clear and present. Beaming bright,
Earth in her August garments virginal
shall infinitely drink the wine of light.

(XXIX)

OTHER POEMS
AUTRES POÈMES

ÉLÉGIE

Je t'ai connue sur une plage du Nord. L'énorme
couchant d'opale et de nacre bramait. Des feux s'allumaient
tout au long de l'infinie digue rectiligne.
Un gueux errait devant les vitres des palaces où l'on dansait.
J'étais plus pauvre que lui, j'étais humble et contrit.
Je ne veux plus me souvenir de ces lieux. Non plus de l'autre mer,
la fameuse indigo avec ses cheveux rouges.
Le luxe nous y caressait le menton de son éventail de palmes,
et les gens avaient pour nous de ces sollicitudes attendries,
complaisantes, satisfaites
que l'on témoigne aux amoureux.
Mois, je savais que tout cela n'était pas pour nous,
mais je t'aimais farouchement à cause
de tes yeux étonnés et de ton drôle de sourire,
et c'était tout, et c'est tout, et aujourd'hui
je veux laisser que loin de nous s'écoulent ces beaux sites
et que s'éteignent les regards qui nous ont vus passer,
et qu'il n'y ait plus de confiance,
que disparaisse à jamais la confiance.
Nulle mer n'a de promesse à tenir. Nul soleil
ne se lève sur un jour plus heureux que la veille. Nulle bouche
ne dit à nulle oreille le moindre mot d'espoir,
et tout est mort avant que d'être né.
Je n'ai jamais connu de vie que dans ce petit souffle
timide et triste que nous portions nous deux entre nos mains
dans l'ombre d'un soir égaré à l'origine
d'une juenesse chancelante,
et cela n'a rapport avec rien, pas même
avec ses persécuteurs. O
amour absolu! Libre, libre misère!
Unique!
C'est te chanter avec exaltation qu'il faudrait comme dans les hymnes
que composaient les fabuleux rois du monde:
les larmes, je crois, te conviennent davantage, les tendres larmes
pareilles à la rosée qui s'assemble, paradoxale,
sur une île dessinée dans l'éternité.
Et je te berce, amour dépouillé, chose sans liens et secrète,
confondue, invisible,
orgueilleuse.
Je te berce, faible pensée.
Je t'endors, tremblant sommeil.

ELEGY

I got to know you on a northern beach. The enormous
sunset, of opal and mother-of-pearl, was moaning. Fires were lit
all along the infinite rectilinear dyke.
A beggar wandered past the windows of the fancy hotels, with the dancing.
I was poorer than he was, I was humble and contrite.
I don't want to remember those places any more. Nor the other sea,
the famous indigo with its red hair.
There luxury caressed us under the chin with its palm-leaf fan,
and people treated us with that tender, complaisant,
        satisfied solicitude
that one observes in lovers.
I myself knew all of that was not for us,
but I loved you fiercely because
of your astonished eyes and your funny smile,
and that was all, and that is all, and today
I want to allow those beautiful places to slip away, far from us,
and those glances, that saw us pass, to be extinguished
and I want there to be no more trust,
let trust disappear for ever.
No sea has a promise to keep. No sun
rises on a day happier than the one before. No mouth
utters the slightest word of hope, no ear receives it,
everything is dead before it is born.
I've never known any life but in this shy sad little
breath we two carried between our hands
in the shade of an evening gone astray at the start
of an unsteady youth,
all of which relates to nothing, not even
to its tormentors. O
absolute love! Unfettered poverty!
Unique!
You should be hymned with exaltation as in the hymns
composed by the world's fabulous kings:
tears, I think, suit you more, tender tears
like the dew that gathers, paradoxical,
on an island sketched in eternity.
And I rock your cradle, love laid bare, a thing secret, untrammelled,
confused, invisible,
proud.
I rock your cradle, tenuous thought.
I put you to sleep, trembling dream.

ODE INFERNALE

Par l'agonie vertige d'être bu,
ravissement, au pied, de disparaître,
ah! qu'il se hait de n'avoir encor su,
cinglant essor de l'instant résolu,
jusqu'où surgit la plénitude d'être!

Cet adieu dur effondre le passé
et se déchire à travers la rupture.
Un battement sur soi-même serré
en quelque azur à sa course opposé
porte en avant les fleurs de la nature.

Écaille ou plume, orgueil vif, ces couleurs
ont la vertu du glas ostentatoire
qui, fascinant, précipitant les heures,
assure enfin le misérable cœur
d'avoir rejoint le cœur de son histoire.

Tout se subsume en l'écartèlement
d'une éternelle et poignante partance.
Penché, versé, défailli, haletant,
l'esprit futur dévore son suspens
dans l'engloutissement qui le balance.

Une seconde encore, et le baiser
du monde au monde assemble en sa détresse
tout un trésor de bonheurs épuisés
pour accomplir ce que n'osa rêver
la plus fervente et prolongée caresse.

Des yeux aux mains un frisson se parcourt
vers l'inconnu de quel fruit, quelle écume,
quelle incréée eau lustrale qui sourd
du noir miracle épais, aveugle et sourd
où le délice à l'excès se consume?

ODE FROM THE UNDERWORLD

Stark vertigo of being swallowed down,
ravishing thrill of vanishing below:
ah! his self-hatred, never having known,
the valiant moment like a slingshot thrown,
how high the plenitude of life can go!

The past is shattered by this hard goodbye
that splits and tears itself across the burst.
A beating wing, compressed in deep blue sky,
the opposite of its trajectory,
bears forward nature's flowers among the first.

Feathers or scales, those tints that proudly burned
are like a tolling bell whose trumpery,
by which the hours are charmed and chased and churned,
assures the grieving heart it has returned
right to the heart of its own history.

All is subsumed within the quartering
of an eternal, poignant setting sail.
Poured out, bent sideways, fainting, sputtering,
the future spirit sups its hovering
in the great gulping-down that holds the scale.

Another moment gone; as one world kisses
another, it collects in its distress
a treasure-chamber of exhausted blisses;
gains what the dream, for all its daring, misses:
dream of the warmest, lengthiest caress.

From eyes to hands there runs a shudder, veering
to the unknown, and to what fruit, what spume,
what uncreated holy water, spearing
from the black miracle, thick, blind, unhearing,
where sweet delight puffs up to self-consume?

Viens donc, désir. Tes images m'entraînent.
Descends, fais-moi descendre au plus profond.
Que ton génie souffle au tournant des veines
et dans l'oreille instille, souveraines,
les choses qui jamais n'ont eu de nom!

L'amant lauré s'extasie du passage
soudain choisi comme un geste d'archet.
Rien ne l'occupe plus que le visage
qui se confond au creux de son voyage
avec la terre à ses mains arrachée.

Lui font cortège en offrande dernière
rochers du soir et cyprès de l'effroi.
Ombre le prend si ne le perd lumière
et seul son pas lui survit, qui s'enferre
dans un assaut de ronces et d'abois.

Mais lui, joyeux et plein de sa musique,
il se délivre aux gouffres effarants
et nageur ivre en haute mer panique,
s'anéantit dans la pensée unique
où lui sourit, à son tour, le néant.

Étrange étreinte où plus rien ne demeure
de qui jadis enchantait les forêts,
mais ne faut-il qu'à jamais l'un se meure
pour qu'effacée, l'autre, de sa pâleur,
se ressuscite en quelque antre sacré?

Amour de mort t'exhume, belle face,
et te désenténèbre lentement.
Ouvre les yeux, dormeuse, sombre espace,
forme de nuit, puis t'invente à voix basse
l'effusion d'un soupir délirant.

Come then, desire. I track your images.
Come down, show me the lowest layerings.
Waft in the windings of my arteries,
blow in my ear, breathe in its passages
the old, supreme, sublimely nameless things.

The laurelled lover thrills to the advance,
incisive as the downstroke of a bow.
Nothing compels him like that countenance,
lost at his lowest point of transience,
mixed with the earth his hands perforce let go.

Last offering: see, to keep him company,
rocks of the evening, cypresses of dread:
light loses him, shade seizes him, maybe;
only his step survives, in battery
of briars and bestial howling closeted.

He bursts with music and with bright emotion,
he plunges in the gulfs that terrify;
a drunken swimmer on a panic ocean,
he seeks oblivion in the single notion
that greets him with the smile of nullity.

A strange embrace! Of him who long before
had charmed the woods, no vestiges remain:
yet surely he must die for evermore,
so she, whom he wipes blank, his pale encore,
deep in some sacred cave may rise again?

The love of death exhumes you, lovely face,
from pools of hollow gloom so slow to go.
Open your eyes: wake, sleeper, shady space,
night-figure; then invent in muted bass
a half-crazed sigh's effusive tremolo.

LA MAIN

La main, son écriture, sa caresse,
la main qui se pose, comme un oiseau,
la main qui s'ouvre, comme une parole,
la main qui parle, comme une marée montante,
la main.

La mort, sa surprise, sa douceur,
la mort qui se promène, comme une fille,
la mort qui sourit, comme une sainte,
la mort qui a raison, comme une reine,
la mort.

Donne la main à la mort,
la main, la mort, qu'elles aillent
ensemble
très loin.

L'ÉTÉ

L'été, l'été, la course à cheval dans la nuit chaude,
un corps de femme sous la moustiquaire,
respirer la rue après le délire du concert,
puis le vagabondage dans la sueur d'alcool,
toute une jeunesse enfouie sous des feuillages tropicaux,
sous le sable que pousse un vent de forge,
et plus jamais nous ne danserons le shimmy aux lanternes,
tu te rappelles, jeunesse?
Le shimmy, une danse des rues de juillet,
et l'avenir dans tes bras comme une boule de feu,
tu te rappelles ce vieil avenir? il s'est pourri,
une pomme rouillée, un cœur qui craque sous le doigt,
l'été, l'été profond, sa voix terrible de contralte,
l'été, pourquoi?

THAT HAND

That hand, its signature, its caress,
that hand settling, like a bird,
that hand opening, like a word,
that hand speaking, like a rising tide,
that hand.

Death, its surprise, its softness,
death out walking, like a girl,
death smiling, like a saint,
death knowing best, like a queen,
death.

Give death that hand,
death, that hand, let them go
together
far away.

SUMMER

Summer, summer, the horserace in the hot night,
a woman's body under the mosquito-net,
breathing the street after the ecstatic concert,
then the forays in the sweat of alcohol,
a whole span of youth buried under tropical foliage,
under the sand driven by a furnace wind,
and never again shall we shimmy by lantern-light,
you remember, my youth?
the shimmy, a street dance in July,
and the future in your arms like a fireball,
you remember that old future? it went bad,
a rusty apple, a heart cracking in your fingers,
summer, deep summer, its fearsome contralto voice,
summer, for what?

LE JOUR

Le jour était brûlant comme un lit de malade.
Le cœur du jour battait à coups précipités.
C'était un jour entre les jours, livide et fade,
un pauvre jour d'un vieil été.

Et l'heure était la plus défaillante des heures,
de toutes les heures de ce jour languissant.
Et vous marchiez à mes côtés comme la peur
près des premiers pas d'un enfant.

Pour me garder du souffle bas du marécage
qui nous suivait grondant, vous me prîtes la main
et me dîtes, levant sur moi vos yeux d'orage:
«Il n'y a pas de lendemain.»

Votre voix résonna, sinistre, dans le site
où je ne trouvais plus le chemin des amants,
puis souriante, à mon oreille, vous reprîtes
dans un calme chuchotement:

«À partir d'aujourd'hui l'éternité commence.
Les rêves révolus, les envols abolis
sont retombés au fond sans fond du noir silence
et de l'imperturbable nuit.

– Quoi! m'écriai-je alors, eh quoi! c'est vous, si chère,
qui m'accablez de tant d'étonnante rigueur
et refusez de voir, fût-ce une fois dernière,
ce que peut un cœur sur un cœur.

Dans quel réduit me plongez-vous de jours sans âge,
pareils à celui-ci qui dure en s'oubliant?
Rien n'aura plus de nom. Jusqu'à votre visage
me sera présence et néant.

J'ai connu l'art secret de persuader l'âme
au point qu'elle s'égale aux volontés d'un dieu.
Devenez dans mes bras la plus femme des femmes
qu'eussent pu séduire mes vœux:

THE DAY

The day burnt like a sick man's bed.
The day's heart raced, its pulse was fast.
Poor day like others, dull as lead:
        summer was nearly past.

The hour was weak as you walked near,
the weakest of that day that ailed;
and you were at my side, like fear
        at the first steps of a child.

The marsh-wind blew behind us and
scolded. Fierce-eyed, you sheltered me,
and told me, as you took my hand:
        'Tomorrow shall not be'.

Your tone of voice put me in fear:
I could not find the lovers' track.
You smiled, love, whispering in my ear,
        bringing the calm note back:

'Today begins eternity.
Dreams overturned, discarded flight,
fall into black infinity
        and unrelenting night.'

'What's this!' I cried: 'how cruelly
you weigh me down! Can this be you,
refusing, even now, to see
        what heart on heart can do?

You plunge me deep in ageless days
like this, oblivious, durable.
Names shall dissolve; your very face
        shall be my nil, my all.

Mine are the arts that sway the soul
to vie with gods whose will is done.
Be the most womanly of all
        the women I could have won:

la mort. Je vous en prie, cédez à mes caresses.
Soyez enfin la mort. Je vous enlacerai
dans un réseau serré d'appels et de tendresses,
        et d'un baiser vous me tuerez.»

Vous m'avez regardé ni moins ni plus amère,
et j'ai lu dans vos yeux le signe qui dit non.
À l'ombre à tout jamais condamnée à se taire
        plus rien sur terre ne répond.

be Death. O yield to my caress:
be Death at last: I'll weave you this
tight net of pleas and tenderness;
        you'll kill me with a kiss.'

Your eye, not more unkind, nor less,
gave me the signal that denies.
When a shade's damned to speechlessness,
        nothing on earth replies.

ANGÈLE

Les magasins se pressent des deux côtés de la rue, et les enseignes, et les plaques de bureaux et d'offices. «Pas de place pour moi dans tout cela», disait Angèle. C'était une fille mal vêtue et seule au monde. Juste, dans son sac, de quoi acheter le journal pour la page des offres d'emploi. Quand elle était petite, elle s'installait dans la pièce la plus reculée, une pièce sans fenêtre, sous la table, à lueur d'une chandelle posée sur une chaise près d'elle, à sa hauteur, et là, tout l'après-midi, jouait à des choses imaginaires. Rien que le grignotement d'une souris l'accompagnait dans son jeu. Mais depuis lors, même plus ce refuge. Depuis lors, la rue, et nulle pièce obscure au bout, obscure, capitonnée, et son odeur de plancher poussiéreux. Chacun des passants qui la croissaient paraissait affairé, chacun avait sa place dans la vie. Qui n'a pas sa place dans la vie ne la trouve que dans le vent. Que de souvenirs habitent le vent! Tout ce qu'on ne sait pas, il en charge sa mémoire. *Maison fondée en 1835*. Depuis 1835, de père en fils, les maîtres de cette maison ont accumulé une science prodigieuse, et leurs clients et leurs voisins peuvent la feuilleter. Tous ces gens se connaissent et ils échangent leurs connaissances. Mais le vent a recueilli le reste, qui est plus grand que la ville entière. Le vent a recuilli toutes les pensées d'Angèle. Seul, le vent.

ANGELA

The shops press in on both sides of the roads, and the signboards, and the name-plates of businesses and offices. 'No room for me in all this,' said Angela. She was a badly-dressed girl and alone in the world. Just enough in her bag to buy the newspaper for the jobs page. When she was little she used to settle herself in the furthest room, a windowless room, under the table, lit by a candle placed on a chair close by, at her own height, and there play imaginary games all afternoon. Only the squeaking of a mouse kept her company in her game. But since then, not even that refuge. Since then, the street, and no obscure room at the far end, obscure, flock-wallpapered, with its smell of dusty floor. Everyone who passed by her seemed busy, everyone had their place in life. One who has no place in life finds it only in the wind. What memories inhabit the wind! All that is not known, the wind stores up in its memory. Established 1835. Since 1835, from father to son, the masters of this business have built up a prodigious fund of knowledge, and their clients and neighbours can dip into it. All these people know each other and exchange what they know. But the wind has gathered up the remainder, which is greater than the entire town. The wind has collected up all Angela's thoughts. Only the wind.

JOURS DE TURIN

Jours de Turin, arcades lumineuses,
stores profonds des boutiques heureuses,
je ne sais pas quand je vous ai perdus.
Qui le saurait? Ne le sait nul non plus.
Le monde était hilare de splendeur,
et je venais, morfondu promeneur,
rêvant d'y être admis comme les autres.
Ô mes cités trompeuses, c'est ma faute.
J'étais marqué d'un destin étranger,
et la mort seule est ma ville à jamais.

LE GESTE

Le geste que tu viens de faire
perce, à l'autre bout de la terre,
le plus abandonné des cœurs.

La lettre que tu viens d'écrire
à qui? fera chez qui? jaillir
le plus désespéré des pleurs.

Le mot que ta bouche a perdu
va dans une nuit inconnue
lever un trouble cauchemar.

Du coup d'une vaine pensée
qui t'a par hasard traversé
une âme est morte quelque part.

DAYS OF TURIN

Days of Turin, arcaded mornings,
bright shops with your commodious awnings,
when did I let you get away?
Who knows? There's no-one left to say.
The world was dressed for revelry;
I came, a star-struck passer-by,
dreaming I too could pass inside.
Perfidious cities! I aimed wide.
For me there was a stranger's fate in store:
death is my only city, evermore.

THE GESTURE

The gesture you made recently
stabs, at earth's far extremity,
a heart in depths of desolation.

The letter that you wrote just now
makes tears – I don't know whose, or how –
well up in total desperation.

The single word your lips let go
enters a night we do not know
and puts a nightmare into play.

Because an idle thought and vain
has passed at random through your brain,
somewhere a soul has passed away.

TRISTESSE DU MIROIR DÉFORMANT

Après la rêverie sur le pont et la rive,
au chevet du soleil mourant,
il n'est dans la cité plus une âme qui vive,
ni dans l'âme un seul revenant.

Les souvenirs ont fait silence, et les voyages,
et le mal d'avoir, tant d'années,
traîné un fastueux et pesant héritage
d'images et de destinées.

Repliez-vous, pays de soie couleur d'orange.
Résumez-vous, célestes plis.
Une plaie au cumul des enfances étranges
ouvre un noir asile d'oubli.

Toutes les nuits du monde en une seule encloses,
dans l'étroit de ces pics dressés,
comme un pleur épaissi le lourd limon déposent
de toutes les mers dissipées.

À cette heure épuisée un creux et long, très long
soupir d'un créateur terrible,
telle une voix sans timbre, enfle l'assomption
d'une prunelle inextinguible.

Elle voit tristement s'élever des machines
de fers en flamme et de bras tors
qui l'emportent au bord de géantes narines
renversées comme chez les morts.

Les cheveux mal cousus au front des vierges folles
se lient aux piloris qu'implique
dans ses nœuds délirants le désertique envol
des draperies salomoniques.

SADNESS OF THE DISTORTING MIRROR

After the dream on bridge and stream
        at the deathbed of the sun,
there isn't a soul left in the town,
        nor a ghost in the soul, not one.

Memories are hushed, and voyages,
        and the pain of having towed
all those destinies and images,
        a proud, heavy, ancient load.

Orange-silk countries, fold away,
        and heavenly folds, fall back:
a wound in the pile of strange child's-play
        opens a refuge of black:

all the nights of the world in one night sealed,
        in the mountains' narrows and screes,
deposit their load like a sob congealed,
        heavy mud of the squandered seas.

A creator grim as a toneless voice
        with a long, long, hollow sigh
inflates the climb, at this worn-out time,
        of an unextinguished eye.

It sees the sad machines that rise,
        bent arms and iron bars burned,
that lift it to giant nasal passages,
        like those of a corpse, upturned.

Mad virgins' forelocks tangle and tie
        to the pillories, folded tight
in the Solomonian drapery,
        raving knots on a desert flight.

«Il faut bien rire un peu», disaient les vieilles femmes
assises devant la maison
aux fenêtres fermées telle une tête infâme
en porte à faux sur son aplomb.

Tête sourde, hantée de clameurs discordantes,
aveugle et zébrée de reflets,
tête tranchée à ras du roc, tête saignante,
chef sans porte, porte sans clef.

In front of the house the old crones said
'Laugh, that's the thing to do.'
With windows shut it was like a head,
notorious, out of true.

Head haunted by jarring cries, deaf head,
head dazzled, blind, striate;
cut-off, erased head, bleeding head,
gateless head, keyless gate.

CORPS

Corps à corps. Un corps
pour un corps. Deux béatitudes sont là,
dont chacune à l'autre lance
son enlacement.
L'âme du monde s'est faite
lumière, et la lumière se divise
en deux chairs d'un égal instant.
Perdus sont les innommables:
absente est l'absence, et noir
le noir de la nuit.
Je tiens la couleur, l'espace, l'électricité,
toute chose, telle et telle,
toute chose universelle,
ô souveraine raison!

Dans le bois toufu de la raison, je suscite la beauté.
Les genoux ployés se nouent
vers l'offertoire inextricable.
Je vois et je veux,
je touche pour naître,
et tu me dis: toi.
D'un réseau de torsades et de reflets, d'un entrelacs
d'écumes jaillit Amour, son épaule pure,
son flanc, sa splendeur,
et sa chevelure
que baise le vent,
Amour, comme une pierre neuve et sainte,
comme un oiseau.
Amour, sommeil fertile, image des images,
créature de l'un et de l'autre, tissu
partout couru de sursauts chatoyants: les caresses,
ciel ponctué, semis de frissons, pluie qui tombe
à l'infini sur le silence des yeux clos,
iris après l'orage, âge sans âge, étoile
de sinueux contours, suavement, qui monte
dans l'unanimité de l'étreinte étirée,
violon d'agonie exquise, long breuvage
de larmes convulsées, visage de l'aurore,
forme! Salut, forme, suprême adieu du monde!

BODY

Body on body. A body
for a body. Two beatitudes exist,
each of which launches at the other
its enlacing.
The soul of the world has become
light, and the light divides
into two fleshes at one same instant.
Lost is the unnameable:
absent is absence, and black
the black of night.
I hold colour, space, electricity,
every thing, this, that,
every universal thing,
o sovereign reason!

In the thick wood of reason, I arouse the beautiful.
The bended knees interlock
to the inextricable prayer.
I see, I desire,
I touch to be born,
and you say to me: you.
From a network of twists and reflexes, from an interlacing
of foams Love wells up, its perfect shoulder,
its flank, its splendour
and its hair
kissed by the wind,
Love, like a stone new and holy,
like a bird.
Love, fertile sleep, image of images,
creation of one and the other, tissue
shot through with glistening leaps: the caresses,
pierced sky, seedbed of shudders, rain falling
endlessly on the silence of closed eyes,
rainbow after storm, age without age, star
of curved contours, softly, that climbs
in the harmony of the drawn-out embrace,
violin of exquisite agony, long draught
of tears convulsing, face of dawn,
form! I greet you, form, the world's supreme farewell!

CHEZ MOI

Chez moi, dans ma mémoire, les soirées
        sont plus dorées qu'ailleurs
et mes regards ne font que rencontrer
        les regards du bonheur.

Tout est à moi dont je vois le visage
        et me parle la voix.
Que m'importent les autres paysages?
        Moi, pareil à ce roi

qui se disait de ses douleurs le maître,
        je suis, dans mes plaisirs,
seul à commander et seul à connaître
        qu'ils ne peuvent périr.

Les biens d'autrui ne sont que cimetières,
        poudre, temples romains.
Distant des morts, je fais valoir mes terres
        et me lave les mains.

Ce que dans leur pays on nomme gloire
        n'amuse que le temps.
Mes souvenirs par contre ont une histoire
        que sans cesse j'entends.

Je me la conte à ma vitre et contemple
        mes secrets horizons,
mes firmaments navigables et l'ample
        pouvoir de mes saisons.

Je me repais des couleurs étrangères
        et des mots inconnus
dont toute chose à moi seul familière
        s'est pour moi revêtue.

Le soir venu, je vais, de porte en porte,
        mes heures visiter,
comme en enfant que l'acceuil réconforte
        de quelque sœur aînée.

CHEZ MOI

Chez moi, in my memories, the evenings are gold
as in no other place
and I gaze at happiness only, and hold
its gaze, face to face.

I possess whatever I see face to face,
voices heard, uttering.
Why should I care for some other place?
I am like that king

who said he was master of all his troubles.
In my own pleasures I
am the sole commander, and I alone know
they never can die.

The riches of others are burial-grounds,
Roman temples and sands.
Set apart from the dead, I farm my own fields
and I wash my hands.

That which in their country is known as glory
can please only time.
By contrast my memories have their story
that I hear all the time.

At my window I spell it out as I study
my secret horizons,
my navigable firmaments, and the ample
power of my seasons.

I take in a feast of unknown words
and outlandish colour,
all flaunted for me, by things that to me
alone are familiar.

In the evening I go and call on my hours,
a door-to-door visitor,
like a child being welcomed and comforted
by an elder sister.

Chacune garde encore une surprise
à montrer à l'enfant,
une pensée qu'il n'avait pas comprise
alors, sur le moment,

une promesse, une aurore, un mystère,
un espoir endormi,
et ce chagrin qui pleura sans lumière
durant combien de nuits?

Et les amours! Jusqu'à celles qui furent
à peine imaginées,
mes heures m'en dévoilent la figure ...
Une, sur l'oreiller:

«Te souviens-tu?» lui dis-je. Elle soupire:
«Mon cœur est toujours là.
Il a toujours quelque chose à te dire.
Écoute comme il bat.

Viens, penche-toi plus près sur ma présence.
Un cœur, c'est bien assez
pour faire, dans l'immense inexistence,
vivre l'éternité.»

And, still, each one of them keeps for the child
        a surprise they can show,
a thought that it hadn't yet understood
        till a moment ago,

a promise, a dawn and a mystery,
        a hope wrapped in slumber,
and the pain that was weeping where no lights shone
        for nights without number.

And the loves! Even some that I scarcely imagined,
        hardly pictured at all:
My hours uncover their faces for me:
        'Perhaps you recall … ?'

I say, on the pillow. She murmurs. 'My heart
        is here every day:
and it always wants to be talking to you.
        Hear it beating away.

Come, close to my presence, lean over me here.
        A heart can contrive
very well, in the vast non-existence, to keep
        eternity live.'

JEAN CASSOU – poet, novelist, essayist, creator of France's National Museum of Modern Art, art critic and public figure – was born in 1987 in Spain to a Spanish mother (his father's mother was Mexican) and as a young man translated, and wrote on, poetry. The shock of war made Cassou a major poet. He moved south to the 'free zone' where he joined (and later led) the Resistance in Toulouse, and wrote the poetic sequence 'The Rose and the Wine'. Upon his arrest and imprisonment in 1941, he composed his '33 Sonnets'. Decorated by de Gaulle at the Liberation, he became president of the National Writers' Committee and of the Union of Intellectuals.

In 1949, he became Director of the National Museum of Modern Art and was the main builder of its great collection. He organised many exhibitions, and wrote copiously on art with great knowledge and insight. An outspoken public figure, he died in 1986, loaded with honours.

TIMOTHY ADÈS was born in midwinter 1941, while Jean Cassou was in prison writing these sonnets. He studied classical literature and international business management. He was a management consultant, then a local voluntary worker. As a poetry translator, Timothy Adès tends to work with rhyme and metre. His first book, Victor Hugo's *How to be a Grandfather*, was published in 2002. He also won awards for *Homer in Cuernavaca* by Alfonso Reyes, and *Against the Grain* by Robert Desnos, writing like Jean Cassou as a wartime resistant.

ALISTAIR ELLIOT was born in Liverpool in 1932 and after living in England, America (during the Second World War), Scotland, Oxford, London, Keele, Shiraz (Iran) and Perugia, has settled in Newcastle. He has translated from Greek (*Medea*), Latin (*Roman Food Poems*, forthcoming), Italian (*Italian Landscape Poems*), German (Heine's Lazarus poems) and French (*French Love Poems*, Valéry's *La jeune parque* and Verlaine's *Femmes / Hombres*). He has published six books of his own poems.

Also available in the
Arc Publications
'VISIBLE POETS' SERIES
(Series Editor: Jean Boase-Beier)

No. 1
MIKLÓS RADNÓTI
(Hungary)
Camp Notebook
TRANSLATED BY FRANCIS JONES
INTRODUCED BY GEORGE SZIRTES

No. 2
BARTOLO CATTAFI
(Italy)
Anthrcacite
TRANSLATED BY BRIAN COLE
INTRODUCED BY PETER DALE
(Poetry Book Society Recommended Translation)

No. 3
MICHAEL STRUNGE
(Denmark)
A Virgin from a Chilly Decade
TRANSLATED BY BENTE ELSWORTH
INTRODUCED BY JOHN FLETCHER

No. 4
TADEUSZ RÓZEWICZ
(Poland)
recycling
TRANSLATED BY BARBARA PLEBANEK & TONY HOWARD
INTRODUCED BY ADAM CZERNIAWSKI

No. 5
CLAUDE DE BURINE
(France)
Words Have Frozen Over
TRANSLATED BY MARTIN SORRELL
INTRODUCED BY SUSAN WICKS

No. 6
CEVAT ÇAPAN
(Turkey)

Where Are You, Susie Petschek?

TRANSLATED BY CEVAT ÇAPAN & MICHAEL HULSE
INTRODUCED BY A. S. BYATT

No. 8
ARJEN DUINKER
(Holland)

A Random Amount of Droplets

TRANSLATED BY WILLEM GROENEWEGEN
INTRODUCED BY JEFFREY WAINWRIGHT